BUILDING BASIC
Math Skills

AGS Publishing
Circle Pines, Minnesota 55014-1796
800-328-2560

\

© 2003 AGS Publishing
4201 Woodland Road, Circle Pines, MN 55014-1796
800-328-2560
www.agsnet.com

AGS Publishing is a trademark of American Guidance Service, Inc.

Printed in the United States of America
ISBN 0-7854-3356-2
Product Number 93691
A 0 9 8 7 6 5

CONTENTS

LESSON 1 Place Value

KEY WORDS

Digit
one of the characters used to write a numeral

Place value
amount a digit is worth based on where it is in a numeral

A **digit** is one of the characters used to write a numeral. Digits used to write numerals are 0, 1, 2, 3, 4, 5, 6, 7, 8, 9. Most numerals have more than one digit. **Place value** is the amount a digit is worth based on where it is in a numeral.

Example | What is the place value of **7** in 37519?

Step 1: Make a place value chart.

Hundred-millions	Ten-millions	Millions	Hundred-thousands	Ten-thousands	Thousands	Hundreds	Tens	Ones

Step 2: Write the numeral 37519 in the chart. Write the numeral in the ones place first.

Hundred-millions	Ten-millions	Millions	Hundred-thousands	Ten-thousands	Thousands	Hundreds	Tens	Ones
				3	7	5	1	9

Step 3: Read the name of the column that holds **7**.

Hundred-millions	Ten-millions	Millions	Hundred-thousands	Ten-thousands	Thousands	Hundreds	Tens	Ones
				3	7	5	1	9

The digit 7 is in the **thousands** place.

A

Write the name of the place for each underlined digit. Use the place value chart.

Place Value Chart

Hundred-millions	Ten-millions	Millions	Hundred-thousands	Ten-thousands	Thousands	Hundreds	Tens	Ones

1. 482957   _____

2. 7901528   _____

3. 82709564   _____

4. 17263   _____

5. 64983000   _____

6. 551290874   _____

7. 4310652   _____

8. 168954   _____

9. 9450*7*161   _____

10. 21705296   _____

11. 874905342   _____

12. 95036   _____

B

Underline the digit that is in the place named.

1. 89456   (thousands)

2. 36804   (hundreds)

3. 4067913   (ten thousands)

4. 605183   (ones)

5. 785084537   (hundred millions)

6. 5806145   (ten thousands)

7. 6783912   (tens)

8. 912463078   (ten millions)

9. 47295036   (hundred thousands)

10. 5490132   (thousands)

11. 98063   (hundreds)

12. 671595003   (ten millions)

LESSON 2   Rounding

KEY WORDS

Rounding
renaming a number
as a simpler number

Rounding a number is renaming it as a simpler number. Numbers are often rounded to the nearest place. The place value chart will help you round numbers.

Example   Round 458,692 to the thousands place.

Hundred-millions	Ten-millions	Millions	Hundred-thousands	Ten-thousands	Thousands	Hundreds	Tens	Ones

Step 1: Find the place you are rounding to.

458,692   Thousands place

Step 2: Look at the digit to its right.

458,692   The digit to its right is **6**.

Step 3: If the digit to its right is 5 or more, add 1 to the place you are rounding to. If the digit is less than 5, do not add anything.

459,692   Since 6 is more than 5, add 1 to the 8 in thousands place.

Step 4: Change all of the digits to the right of the place to which you are rounding to zeros.

459,000   The digits in hundreds, tens, and ones place become zeros.

458,692 rounded to the thousands place is **459,000**.

A. Round these numbers to the nearest tens place.

1. 47,134 _____

2. 98 _____

3. 516,764 _____

4. 652,867 _____

5. 195,039,796 _____

6. 532,161 _____

RULES TO REMEMBER

■ A **rounded number** is close to the real number.

■ A **rounded number** always ends with zero.

B. Round these numbers to the nearest thousands place.

1. 750,835 _____

2. 3,281,523 _____

3. 628,874 _____

4. 7,896 _____

5. 5,410,342 _____

6. 63,029 _____

C. Complete the chart by rounding to the place named.

		Tens	Hundreds	Thousands
1.	6,814			
2.	3,904,736			
3.	23,871			
4.	5,362,817			
5.	80,435,689			

LESSON 3   Adding Whole Numbers

KEY WORDS

Addition
combining numbers
to find their total

Addend
a number being added
to another number

Order
to arrange from
smallest to largest

Sum
the answer to an
addition problem

Zero
the first whole
number

Addition is combining numbers to find a total, or **sum**. The numbers that are added are called **addends.** The **order** in which two numbers are added does not change the sum. Adding **zero** to a number does not change the number.

Example Beth worked 7 hours today. She worked 8 hours yesterday. How many hours did she work altogether?

Step 1: Set up an addition problem. The addends are 7 and 8.

$7 + 8 =$

Step 2: To use the number line, start with the larger number. Add the smaller number onto it.

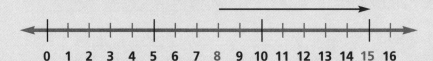

Step 3: You end on 15. The sum of 7 and 8 is 15.

Beth worked **15** hours altogether.

The order of addends does not change their sum.
The sum is the same when you add $9 + 4$ or $4 + 9$.

$9 + 4 = 13$

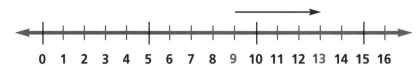

$4 + 9 = 13$

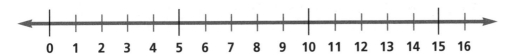

RULES TO REMEMBER

- Line up the addends by the ones column.
- When adding two-digit numbers, add the ones first.

A Use the number line to find each sum.

1. 9	**2.** 3	**3.** 6	**4.** 7	**5.** 1	**6.** 0	**7.** 5
+ 2	+ 5	+ 9	+ 6	+ 4	+ 8	+ 4

8. 2	**9.** 8	**10.** 5	**11.** 8	**12.** 5	**13.** 7	**14.** 3
+ 9	+ 6	+ 7	+ 8	+ 9	+ 7	+ 3

15. 2	**16.** 9	**17.** 1	**18.** 4	**19.** 6	**20.** 2	**21.** 8
+ 7	+ 9	+ 5	+ 7	+ 5	+ 8	+ 7

Example Dan has 23 CDs. Betty has 36 CDs.
How many CDs do they have together?

Step 1: Set up an addition problem. The addends are 23 and 36.

```
  23
+ 36
```

Step 2: Find the sum of the ones.

```
  23
+ 36
   9
```

Step 3: Find the sum of the tens.

```
  23
+ 36
  59
```

Dan and Betty have a total of **59** CDs.

B Find each sum.

1. 31	**2.** 17	**3.** 48	**4.** 73	**5.** 84	**6.** 27	**7.** 50
+ 44	+ 62	+ 40	+ 25	+ 12	+ 60	+ 29

8. 15	**9.** 25	**10.** 81	**11.** 24	**12.** 19	**13.** 56	**14.** 35
+ 61	+ 73	+ 13	+ 55	+ 40	+ 11	+ 42

15. 68	**16.** 46	**17.** 15	**18.** 79	**19.** 30	**20.** 45	**21.** 26
+ 21	+ 53	+ 72	+ 10	+ 54	+ 31	+ 43

LESSON 4   Adding Two-Digit Numbers with Renaming

KEY WORDS

Rename
to write a number as groups of ones and tens

Sometimes a number needs to be **renamed** to complete the addition. When a number is renamed, it is written as tens and ones.

Example   Rico worked 38 hours this week. He worked 35 hours last week. How many hours did he work during the past two weeks?

Step 1: Set up an addition problem. The addends are 38 and 35. The addends are written with the ones lined up.

$$\begin{array}{r} 38 \\ + 35 \\ \hline \end{array}$$

Step 2: Find the sum of the ones.

$$\begin{array}{r} 38 \\ + 35 \\ \hline \end{array} \qquad 8 + 5 = 13$$

Step 3: Rename 13 ones as 1 ten and 3 ones. Write the 3 in the ones column. Write the 1 in the tens column.

$$\begin{array}{r} 1 \\ 38 \\ + 35 \\ \hline 3 \end{array}$$

Step 4: Find the sum of the tens.

$$\begin{array}{r} 1 \\ 38 \\ + 35 \\ \hline 73 \end{array}$$

Rico worked **73** hours.

 Write each number as groups of tens and ones.

1. 78 _____ tens and _____ ones

2. 49 _____ tens and _____ ones

3. 56 _____ tens and _____ ones

4. 32 _____ tens and _____ ones

5. 14 _____ tens and _____ ones

6. 95 _____ tens and _____ ones

7. 63 _____ tens and _____ ones

8. 81 _____ tens and _____ ones

9. 25 _____ tens and _____ ones

10. 47 _____ tens and _____ ones

B Find each sum.

1. 36 + 45	**2.** 73 + 28	**3.** 80 + 27	**4.** 77 + 15	**5.** 49 + 12
6. 53 + 36	**7.** 41 + 29	**8.** 16 + 85	**9.** 63 + 25	**10.** 19 + 52
11. 37 + 44	**12.** 60 + 50	**13.** 22 + 39	**14.** 91 + 27	**15.** 39 + 49
16. 11 + 82	**17.** 85 + 33	**18.** 26 + 75	**19.** 46 + 41	**20.** 71 + 55
21. 92 + 10	**22.** 55 + 41	**23.** 46 + 42	**24.** 81 + 14	**25.** 17 + 62

LESSON 5   Problem Solving with Addition

KEY WORDS

Word problem
sentences that describe
a math problem

A **word problem** is a group of sentences that describes a math problem. Read the sentences and then write the addition problem.

Example   Lilly bowled two games. Her scores were 138 and 152. Max also bowled two games. He knocked down 27 more pins than Lilly. What was Max's total score for the two games?

Step 1: State the question you must answer. This is often found at the end of a word problem. The question you must answer for this problem is *What was Max's total score for the two games?*

Step 2: Make a list of the information you are given.

Lilly bowled two games.
She scored 138 and 152.
Max bowled two games.
He knocked down 27 more pins than Lilly.

Step 3: Make a plan to solve the problem.

1. Find Lilly's total.
2. Add 27 to that sum to find Max's total.

Step 4: Follow your plan.

```
   1           1
  138         290
+ 152        + 27
 -----       -----
  290         317
```

Max's total score was **317**.

 Use the steps to solve each word problem.

Tia drove 148 miles on Monday. She drove 218 miles on Tuesday. She has 76 more miles to drive. What is the total number of miles Tia will drive rounded to the tens place?

1. State the question you must answer.

_____

_____

2. List what you know.

_____

_____

3. Make a plan to solve the problem.

_____

_____

4. Follow your plan.

Luke earned $135.00 last week. He earned $178.00 this week. Bud earned $56.00 more than Luke's total. How much did Bud earn during the past two weeks?

5. State the question you must answer.

_____

_____

6. List what you know.

_____

_____

7. Make a plan to solve the problem.

_____

_____

8. Follow your plan.

B Use the same steps to solve these problems.

1. There are 45,819 people living in Centerville. There are 18,355 people living in Oakdale. What is the total number of people living in each city rounded to the nearest thousand?

2. A recycling center received 459 cans on Monday. On Wednesday, the center received 718 cans. The center received 22 more cans on Saturday than on Monday. In all, how many cans did the center receive during those three days?

LESSON 6   Subtraction

KEY WORDS

Subtraction
taking one number
away from another to
find the difference

Difference
the answer to a
subtraction problem

Subtraction is taking one number away from another. The answer to a subtraction problem is called the **difference**.

Example   Mel had $17.00. He spent $6.00 on lunch.
How much money does Mel have now?

Step 1: Set up a subtraction problem. Start with the larger number. Write the smaller number below it.

```
  17
-  6
----
```

Step 2: Find the difference of the digits in the ones place.

```
  17
-  6
----
   1
```

Step 3: Now look at the tens place. Only the top number has a digit in the tens place. There is nothing to take away from this digit. So write it in the tens place in the answer.

```
  17          Check your work by adding.        11
-  6                                           + 6
----                                           ----
  11                                            17
```

Mel now has **$11.00**.

A Find each difference. Check your work by adding.

1. 9 − 3	**2.** 18 − 7	**3.** 19 − 8	**4.** 8 − 5	**5.** 18 − 6	**6.** 15 − 4
7. 15 − 3	**8.** 7 − 5	**9.** 12 − 2	**10.** 13 − 2	**11.** 17 − 5	**12.** 5 − 0
13. 9 − 5	**14.** 4 − 2	**15.** 16 − 4	**16.** 19 − 5	**17.** 16 − 3	**18.** 9 − 4

| **Example** | Jack earned $278.00 this week. He put aside $135.00 for rent. How much money is left? |

Step 1: Set up a subtraction problem. Write the larger number first.

$$\begin{array}{r} 278 \\ -135 \\ \hline \end{array}$$

Step 2: Find the difference of the digits in the ones place.

$$\begin{array}{r} 278 \\ -135 \\ \hline 3 \end{array}$$

Step 3: Find the difference of the digits in the tens place.

$$\begin{array}{r} 278 \\ -135 \\ \hline 43 \end{array}$$

Step 4: Find the difference of the digits in the hundreds place.

$$\begin{array}{r} 278 \\ -135 \\ \hline 143 \end{array}$$ Check your work by adding: $$\begin{array}{r} 143 \\ +135 \\ \hline 278 \end{array}$$

Jack has **$143.00** left.

- When setting up a subtraction problem, write the larger number first.

- Line up the numbers in the ones place.

- Check your subtraction by adding the answer and the middle number. The sum should be the top number.

B Find each difference. Check your work by adding.

1. $\begin{array}{r} 58 \\ -23 \\ \hline \end{array}$ **2.** $\begin{array}{r} 79 \\ -46 \\ \hline \end{array}$ **3.** $\begin{array}{r} 81 \\ -60 \\ \hline \end{array}$ **4.** $\begin{array}{r} 35 \\ -12 \\ \hline \end{array}$ **5.** $\begin{array}{r} 40 \\ -20 \\ \hline \end{array}$ **6.** $\begin{array}{r} 72 \\ -51 \\ \hline \end{array}$

7. $\begin{array}{r} 83 \\ -22 \\ \hline \end{array}$ **8.** $\begin{array}{r} 59 \\ -38 \\ \hline \end{array}$ **9.** $\begin{array}{r} 75 \\ -25 \\ \hline \end{array}$ **10.** $\begin{array}{r} 98 \\ -37 \\ \hline \end{array}$ **11.** $\begin{array}{r} 184 \\ -74 \\ \hline \end{array}$ **12.** $\begin{array}{r} 987 \\ -615 \\ \hline \end{array}$

13. $\begin{array}{r} 650 \\ -40 \\ \hline \end{array}$ **14.** $\begin{array}{r} 753 \\ -642 \\ \hline \end{array}$ **15.** $\begin{array}{r} 682 \\ -70 \\ \hline \end{array}$ **16.** $\begin{array}{r} 456 \\ -311 \\ \hline \end{array}$ **17.** $\begin{array}{r} 571 \\ -240 \\ \hline \end{array}$ **18.** $\begin{array}{r} 779 \\ -673 \\ \hline \end{array}$

19. $\begin{array}{r} 840 \\ -530 \\ \hline \end{array}$ **20.** $\begin{array}{r} 445 \\ -312 \\ \hline \end{array}$ **21.** $\begin{array}{r} 506 \\ -102 \\ \hline \end{array}$ **22.** $\begin{array}{r} 837 \\ -215 \\ \hline \end{array}$ **23.** $\begin{array}{r} 941 \\ -341 \\ \hline \end{array}$ **24.** $\begin{array}{r} 755 \\ -421 \\ \hline \end{array}$

LESSON 7   Subtraction with Renaming

KEY WORDS

Rename
to write a number as groups of ones and tens

Numbers sometimes need to be renamed to complete the subtraction. Renaming a number means writing it as a group of ones and tens.

Example   Ali worked 31 hours this week. Dee worked 9 fewer hours than Ali. How many hours did Dee work?

Step 1: Set up a subtraction problem. Start with the larger number. Write the smaller number below it.

```
  31
-  9
```

Step 2: Find the difference between the digits in the ones place. You cannot subtract 9 from 1. You must rename. To rename, write 31 as 2 tens and 11 ones. Then find the difference of 11 and 9.

```
  31            2 11
-  9            3̶1̶
----         -   9
  1          ------
                  2
```

Step 3: Find the difference between the digits in the tens place. Only the top number has a digit in the tens place. There is nothing to take away from this digit. So write 2 in the tens place in the answer.

```
  2 11
  3̶1̶        Check your        22
-  9        work by adding.  + 9
------                      ------
  22                          31
```

Dee worked **22** hours.

A Find each difference. Check your work by adding.

1.	2.	3.	4.	5.	6.
43 − 35	61 − 27	83 − 49	34 − 25	92 − 8	57 − 39

7.	8.	9.	10.	11.	12.
75 − 46	45 − 18	23 − 9	81 − 65	31 − 19	53 − 16

Example   Hillside High made 400 tickets for a play. Students sold 248 of the tickets. How many tickets are left?

Step 1: Set up a subtraction problem. Write the larger number first.

$$\begin{array}{r} 400 \\ -\,248 \\ \hline \end{array}$$

Step 2: Find the difference of the digits in the ones place. Since you cannot take 8 from 0, you must rename. Take 1 from the hundreds place. Rename it as 10 tens. Take 1 from the tens place. Rename it as 10 ones. Subtract 8 from 10.

$$\begin{array}{r} 9 \\ 3\ \cancel{10}\ 10 \\ \cancel{4}\ \cancel{0}\ \cancel{0} \\ -\,2\ 4\ 8 \\ \hline 2 \end{array}$$

Step 3: Find the difference of the digits in the tens place.

$$\begin{array}{r} 9 \\ 3\ \cancel{10}\ 10 \\ \cancel{4}\ \cancel{0}\ \cancel{0} \\ -\,2\ 4\ 8 \\ \hline 5\ 2 \end{array}$$

Step 4: Find the difference of the digits in the hundreds place.

$$\begin{array}{r} 9 \\ 3\ \cancel{10}\ 10 \\ \cancel{4}\ \cancel{0}\ \cancel{0} \\ -\,2\ 4\ 8 \\ \hline 1\ 5\ 2 \end{array}$$

Check your work by adding:
$$\begin{array}{r} 152 \\ +\,248 \\ \hline 400 \end{array}$$

There are **152** tickets left.

B Find each difference. Check your work by adding.

1. $\begin{array}{r} 254 \\ -\,128 \\ \hline \end{array}$ **2.** $\begin{array}{r} 700 \\ -\,465 \\ \hline \end{array}$ **3.** $\begin{array}{r} 381 \\ -\,267 \\ \hline \end{array}$ **4.** $\begin{array}{r} 576 \\ -\,349 \\ \hline \end{array}$ **5.** $\begin{array}{r} 400 \\ -\,281 \\ \hline \end{array}$ **6.** $\begin{array}{r} 972 \\ -\,536 \\ \hline \end{array}$

7. $\begin{array}{r} 803 \\ -\,723 \\ \hline \end{array}$ **8.** $\begin{array}{r} 950 \\ -\,380 \\ \hline \end{array}$ **9.** $\begin{array}{r} 347 \\ -\,255 \\ \hline \end{array}$ **10.** $\begin{array}{r} 418 \\ -\,217 \\ \hline \end{array}$ **11.** $\begin{array}{r} 436 \\ -\,117 \\ \hline \end{array}$ **12.** $\begin{array}{r} 390 \\ -\,185 \\ \hline \end{array}$

LESSON 8 Problem Solving with Subtraction

KEY WORDS

Word problem
sentences that describe a math problem

A **word problem** is a group of sentences that describes a math problem. Read the sentences and then write the subtraction problem.

Example Jon scored 1,487 points on a video game. Lance scored 319 fewer points than Jon. What is their total score rounded to the hundreds place?

Step 1: State the question you must answer. This is often found at the end of a word problem. The question you must answer for this problem is *What is their total score rounded to the hundreds place?*

Step 2: Make a list of the information you are given.

Jon scored 1,487 points.
Lance scored 319 fewer points than Jon.

Step 3: Make a plan to solve the problem.

1. Find Lance's total
2. Find the total number of points they scored altogether.
3. Round the sum to the hundreds place.

Step 4: Follow your plan.

```
      7 17              1 1
   1 4 8̶ 7̶           1 4 8 7          2 6 55 → 2,700
 −     3 1 9        + 1 1 6 8
   ─────────         ─────────
   1 1 6 8            2 6 5 5
```

Their total score rounded to the hundreds place is **2,700** points.

 Use the steps to solve each word problem.

Nick went to the mall with $50.00. He spent $28.00 on pants. He spent $17.00 on a shirt. Before he left the mall, Nick bought lunch for $4.00. How much money did Nick have when he left the mall?

1. State the question you must answer.

_____

_____

2. List what you know.

_____

_____

3. Make a plan to solve the problem.

_____

_____

4. Follow your plan.

A sports shop has 458 pairs of sneakers. During the first day of a sale, shoppers bought 79 pairs of the sneakers. On the second day, shoppers bought 108 pairs of sneakers. How many pairs of sneakers are left?

5. State the question you must answer.

_____

_____

6. List what you know.

_____

_____

7. Make a plan to solve the problem.

_____

_____

8. Follow your plan.

B Use the same steps to solve these problems.

1. The All Star Company has 18,590 workers. The Show Stopper Company has 2,145 fewer workers than the All Star Company. What is the total number of workers at these two companies rounded to the thousands place?

2. On Saturday, a movie theater sold 608 tickets. On Monday, 64 less tickets were sold than on Saturday. On Wednesday, 29 less tickets were sold than on Monday. How many tickets did the theater sell on Wednesday?

RULES TO REMEMBER

- When adding or subtracting, line up the numbers by the ones column.

- Sometimes you need to subtract and then add to solve a word problem.

- Look for the clue words _less than, fewer,_ and _difference._ They often show that you must subtract to solve the problem.

LESSON 9   Multiplication

KEY WORDS

Multiplication
adding one number
to itself many times

Factors
the numbers that
are multiplied

Product
the answer to a
multiplication
problem

Multiplication is adding a number to itself many times. The numbers that are multiplied are called **factors.** The answer to a multiplication problem is called the **product.**

Example   Carol has 6 bags of cookies. There are 8 cookies in each bag. How many cookies does Carol have?

Step 1: Set up a multiplication problem. Write the two factors or numbers you are multiplying.

Factors ⟶ $6 \times 8 =$

Step 2: Use the multiplication chart to find the product. The product is shown in the box where the two factors meet.

x	1	2	3	4	5	6	7	8	9	10
1	1	2	3	4	5	6	7	8	9	10
2	2	4	6	8	10	12	14	16	18	20
3	3	6	9	12	15	18	21	24	27	30
4	4	8	12	16	20	24	28	32	36	40
5	5	10	15	20	25	30	35	40	45	50
6	6	12	18	24	30	36	42	48	54	60
7	7	14	21	28	35	42	49	56	63	70
8	8	16	24	32	40	48	56	64	72	80
9	9	18	27	36	45	54	63	72	81	90
10	10	20	30	40	50	60	70	80	90	100

$6 \times 8 = 48$ ⟵ Product

Carol has **48** cookies.

A   **Use the multiplication chart to find each product.**

1. 9 $\times 6$	**2.** 4 $\times 7$	**3.** 10 $\times 5$	**4.** 7 $\times 7$	**5.** 2 $\times 9$	**6.** 0 $\times 3$
7. 5 $\times 4$	**8.** 8 $\times 7$	**9.** 10 $\times 9$	**10.** 2 $\times 6$	**11.** 9 $\times 9$	**12.** 4 $\times 8$

13. 9 ×1   **14.** 7 ×2   **15.** 6 ×6   **16.** 10 ×10   **17.** 1 ×3   **18.** 7 ×9

Example Beth has 4 photo albums. Each album holds 22 photos. How many photos are in all the albums?

Step 1: Set up a multiplication problem. Write the larger factor first.

$$\begin{array}{r} 22 \\ \times\ 4 \\ \hline \end{array}$$

Step 2: Find the product of the factors in the ones column.

$$\begin{array}{r} 22 \\ \times\ 4 \\ \hline 8 \end{array}$$

Step 3: Find the product of the factors in the tens column.

$$\begin{array}{r} 22 \\ \times\ 4 \\ \hline 88 \end{array}$$

There are **88** photos in the albums.

B Find each product.

1. 13 ×3   **2.** 79 ×1   **3.** 11 ×8   **4.** 30 ×2   **5.** 42 ×2   **6.** 20 ×4

7. 83 ×0   **8.** 14 ×2   **9.** 12 ×4   **10.** 95 ×1   **11.** 11 ×9   **12.** 23 ×3

13. 12 ×3   **14.** 11 ×5   **15.** 68 ×1   **16.** 41 ×2   **17.** 32 ×3   **18.** 11 ×6

LESSON 10 Multiplication with Renaming

Numbers sometimes need to be **renamed** to complete multiplication problems. If the product in the ones column is greater than 9, the product must be renamed.

Example The Sports Shop has 24 boxes of footballs. There are 8 footballs in each box. How many footballs are in all?

Step 1: Set up a multiplication problem. Write the larger factor first.

$$\begin{array}{r} 24 \\ \times\ 8 \\ \hline \end{array}$$

Step 2: Find the product of the digits in the ones column. Since the product is greater than 9, you must rename it.

$$\begin{array}{r} 3 \\ 24 \\ \times\ 8 \\ \hline 2 \end{array}$$

$4 \times 8 = 32$

Rename 32 as **3** tens and **2** ones
Write **2** in **ones** place of the product.
Write **3** above the **tens** place.

Step 3: Find the product of the digits in the tens column. Add the 3. Write the sum in the product.

$$\begin{array}{r} 3 \\ 24 \\ \times\ 8 \\ \hline 192 \end{array}$$

$2 \times 8 = 16$

$16 + 3 = 19$

There are **192** footballs in the boxes.

A Find each product.

1. $\begin{array}{r} 35 \\ \times\ 6 \\ \hline \end{array}$
2. $\begin{array}{r} 54 \\ \times\ 3 \\ \hline \end{array}$
3. $\begin{array}{r} 72 \\ \times\ 5 \\ \hline \end{array}$
4. $\begin{array}{r} 27 \\ \times\ 2 \\ \hline \end{array}$
5. $\begin{array}{r} 13 \\ \times\ 9 \\ \hline \end{array}$
6. $\begin{array}{r} 86 \\ \times\ 2 \\ \hline \end{array}$

7. $\begin{array}{r} 95 \\ \times\ 3 \\ \hline \end{array}$
8. $\begin{array}{r} 28 \\ \times\ 7 \\ \hline \end{array}$
9. $\begin{array}{r} 46 \\ \times\ 4 \\ \hline \end{array}$
10. $\begin{array}{r} 39 \\ \times\ 5 \\ \hline \end{array}$
11. $\begin{array}{r} 14 \\ \times\ 7 \\ \hline \end{array}$
12. $\begin{array}{r} 78 \\ \times\ 3 \\ \hline \end{array}$

13. $\begin{array}{r} 59 \\ \times\ 6 \\ \hline \end{array}$
14. $\begin{array}{r} 17 \\ \times\ 8 \\ \hline \end{array}$
15. $\begin{array}{r} 15 \\ \times\ 9 \\ \hline \end{array}$
16. $\begin{array}{r} 61 \\ \times\ 6 \\ \hline \end{array}$
17. $\begin{array}{r} 19 \\ \times\ 7 \\ \hline \end{array}$
18. $\begin{array}{r} 67 \\ \times\ 4 \\ \hline \end{array}$

The product of one factor and a digit in another factor is called a **partial product**.

Example The Sports Shop also has 36 boxes of baseballs. Each box holds 24 baseballs. How many baseballs are there in all?

Step 1: Set up a multiplication problem. Write the larger factor first.

$$\begin{array}{r} 36 \\ \times\ 24 \\ \hline \end{array}$$

Step 2: Multiply the first factor by the ones digit of the second factor. Write this partial product.

$$\begin{array}{r} 36 \\ \times\ 24 \\ \hline 144 \end{array}$$ ◀———— $36 \times 4 = 144$

Step 3: Put an **0** under the ones digit of the partial product.

$$\begin{array}{r} 36 \\ \times\ 24 \\ \hline 144 \\ 0 \end{array}$$

Step 4: Multiply the first factor by the tens digit of the second factor. Write this partial product under the tens and hundreds digits.

$$\begin{array}{r} 36 \\ \times\ 24 \\ \hline 144 \\ 720 \end{array}$$ ◀———— $36 \times 2 = 72$

Step5: Add the partial products.

$$\begin{array}{r} 36 \\ \times\ 24 \\ \hline 144 \\ 720 \\ \hline 864 \end{array}$$

There are **864** baseballs in all.

B Find each product.

1.	2.	3.	4.	5.	6.
47	93	65	38	29	72
× 18	× 24	× 39	× 54	× 17	× 44

7.	8.	9.	10.	11.	12.
59	26	83	76	19	33
× 28	× 85	× 20	× 14	× 87	× 52

LESSON 11   Problem Solving with Multiplication

KEY WORDS

Word problem
sentences that describe
a math problem

A **word problem** is a group of sentences that describes a math problem.
Read the sentences and then write the multiplication problem.

Example   A drama club sold 128 adult tickets and 89 student tickets
to a play. Each adult ticket cost $5.00. Each student ticket
cost $3.00. What is the total amount of money the club
collected?

Step 1: State the question you must answer. This is often found
at the end of a word problem. The question you must
answer for this problem is *What is the total amount of
money the club collected?*

Step 2: Make a list of the information you are given.

128 adult tickets were sold
89 student tickets were sold
Adult ticket cost $5.00
Student ticket cost $3.00

Step 3: Make a plan to solve the problem.

*1. Multiply the total number of adult tickets sold
by the price of each ticket.*
*2. Multiply the total number of student tickets sold
by the price of each ticket.*
3. Add the products.

Step 4: Follow your plan.

$$\begin{array}{r} 128 \\ \times\ 5 \\ \hline 640 \end{array} \qquad \begin{array}{r} 89 \\ \times\ 3 \\ \hline 267 \end{array} \qquad \begin{array}{r} ^{1} \\ 640 \\ +\ 267 \\ \hline 907 \end{array}$$

The club collected **$907.00**.

 Use the steps to solve each word problem.

A jug of fruit punch holds 144 ounces. Hallie bought 15 jugs
for a party. How many ounces of punch does Hallie have?

1. State the question you must answer.

_____

_____

2. List what you know.

_____

_____

3. Make a plan to solve the problem.

_____

_____

4. Follow your plan.

Rick charges $15.00 to cut a lawn. He charges $18.00 to weed a garden. In June, Rick cut 22 lawns. He also weeded 9 gardens. How much money did Rick make in June?

5. State the question you must answer.

_____

_____

6. List what you know.

_____

_____

7. Make a plan to solve the problem.

_____

_____

8. Follow your plan.

B Use the same steps to solve these problems.

1. A snack bar bought 36 boxes of hot dogs. Each box holds 48 hot dogs. How many hot dogs did the snack bar buy?

2. Every Saturday, Rick delivers 86 newspapers. Every Sunday, he delivers 135 newspapers. There are 52 weeks in a year. How many newspapers does Rick deliver in one year?

LESSON 12   Division

KEY WORDS

Division
finding how many times
a number is contained
in another number

Dividend
the number that
is being divided

Divisor
the number by which
you are dividing

Quotient
the answer to a
division problem

Division is breaking a number into equal groups (parts). The number that is being divided is called the **dividend.** The **divisor** is the number by which you are dividing. The answer to a division problem is called the **quotient.**

Example Adam has 72 trading cards. He split them into 8 equal stacks. How many cards are in each stack?

Step 1: Set up a division problem. First write the dividend or number that is being broken down into smaller groups.

72

Step 2: Put a division sign around the dividend. Outside the division sign, write the divisor or number by which you are dividing.

$8 \overline{)72}$

Step 3: Write the quotient, or answer, above the division sign.

$$9 \leftarrow \text{quotient}$$
$$\text{divisor} \rightarrow 8\overline{)72}$$
$$\uparrow \text{dividend}$$

Check your work by multiplying.

$$\begin{array}{r} 8 \\ \times 9 \\ \hline 72 \end{array}$$

There are **9** cards in each stack.

A Find each quotient.

1. $8\overline{)48}$ **2.** $5\overline{)35}$ **3.** $4\overline{)36}$ **4.** $7\overline{)49}$ **5.** $3\overline{)18}$

6. $6\overline{)24}$ **7.** $2\overline{)18}$ **8.** $5\overline{)25}$ **9.** $9\overline{)81}$ **10.** $6\overline{)42}$

11. $8\overline{)56}$ **12.** $4\overline{)32}$ **13.** $7\overline{)63}$ **14.** $9\overline{)54}$ **15.** $9\overline{)45}$

16. $6\overline{)42}$ **17.** $7\overline{)56}$ **18.** $6\overline{)54}$ **19.** $9\overline{)72}$ **20.** $7\overline{)35}$

| **Example** | Bria has 168 beads. She wants to divide them evenly among 7 jars. How many beads should Bria put in each jar? |

Step 1: Set up a division problem.

$$7\overline{)168}$$

Step 2: See if the divisor can go into the first digit of the dividend.

$7\overline{)168}$ ◄────── 7 cannot go into **1**

Step 3: See if the divisor can go into the first two digits of the dividend.

$$\begin{array}{r} 2 \\ 7\overline{)168} \\ -14 \end{array}$$ ◄────── 7 can go into 16 ◄── 7 × 2 = 14

Step 4: Subtract. Bring down the next digit from the dividend.

$$\begin{array}{r} 2 \\ 7\overline{)168} \\ -14\!\downarrow \\ \hline 28 \end{array}$$

Step 5: See if the divisor can go into the number that formed.

$$\begin{array}{r} 24 \\ 7\overline{)168} \\ -14\!\downarrow \\ \hline 28 \\ -28 \\ \hline 0 \end{array}$$ ◄────── 7 can go into **28** ◄── 7 × 4 = 28

Bria should put **24** beads in each jar.

■ You can check division with multiplication. The divisor times the quotient equals the dividend.

■ Any number divided by 1 equals the number.

■ Any number divided by itself equals 1.

B Find each quotient. Show your work.

1. $5\overline{)155}$ **2.** $8\overline{)136}$ **3.** $3\overline{)192}$ **4.** $7\overline{)322}$ **5.** $4\overline{)340}$

6. $9\overline{)126}$ **7.** $6\overline{)432}$ **8.** $4\overline{)388}$ **9.** $7\overline{)413}$ **10.** $9\overline{)378}$

11. $5\overline{)265}$ **12.** $8\overline{)512}$ **13.** $9\overline{)477}$ **14.** $8\overline{)320}$ **15.** $5\overline{)300}$

LESSON 13   Division with Remainders

KEY WORDS

Remainder
an amount left over
when dividing

In a division problem, the dividend cannot always be divided into equal parts. When this happens, the quotient, or answer, has a remainder. A **remainder** means that there is an amount left over.

Example Dee baked 172 cookies. She will put them in bags holding 3 cookies each. How many bags does Dee need?

Step 1: Set up a division problem. Write the dividend under the division sign. Write the divisor outside the division sign.

$3\overline{)172}$

Step 2: See if the divisor goes into the first digit of the dividend.

$3\overline{)172}$ ◄——— 3 cannot go into **1**

Step 3: See if the divisor can go into the first two digits of the dividend.

$$\begin{array}{r} 5 \\ 3\overline{)172} \\ -15 \end{array}$$ ◄—— 3 can go into 17 ◄— **3 × 5 = 15**

Step 4: Subtract. Bring down the next digit from the dividend.

$$\begin{array}{r} 5 \\ 3\overline{)172} \\ -15\downarrow \\ \hline 22 \end{array}$$

Step 5: See if the divisor can go into the number that formed.

$$\begin{array}{r} 57\ r\ 1 \\ 3\overline{)172} \\ -15\downarrow \\ \hline 22 \end{array}$$

3 can go into **22**   **3 × 7 = 21** ——→ -21

The remainder is **1**. Write **r 1** in ——→ 1
the quotient.

Dee needs **57** bags. She will have **1** cookie left over.

A Find each quotient.

1. $5\overline{)418}$ 2. $6\overline{)325}$ 3. $4\overline{)126}$ 4. $7\overline{)330}$ 5. $3\overline{)158}$

6. $6\overline{)354}$ 7. $2\overline{)187}$ 8. $9\overline{)211}$ 9. $4\overline{)371}$ 10. $6\overline{)255}$

11. $8\overline{)623}$ 12. $4\overline{)296}$ 13. $7\overline{)602}$ 14. $9\overline{)284}$ 15. $5\overline{)427}$

Example

A factory made 3,890 zippers. Ted packs the zippers in boxes. Each box holds 36 zippers. How many boxes does Ted need?

Step 1: Set up a division problem.

$$36\overline{)3{,}890}$$

Step 2: See if the divisor can go into the first digit of the dividend.

$36\overline{)3{,}890}$ ◀— 36 cannot go into **3**

Step 3: See if the divisor can go into the first two digits of the dividend.

$$\begin{array}{r} 1 \\ 36\overline{)3{,}890} \\ -\ 36 \\ \hline \end{array}$$ ◀— 36 can go into 38 ◀ **36 × 1 = 36**

Step 4: Subtract. Bring down the next digit from the dividend.

$$\begin{array}{r} 1 \\ 36\overline{)3{,}890} \\ -\ 36\downarrow \\ \hline 29 \end{array}$$

Step 5: See if the divisor can go into the number that formed.

$$\begin{array}{r} 1 \\ 36\overline{)3{,}890} \\ -\ 36 \\ \hline 29 \end{array}$$ ◀— 36 cannot go into **29**

Step 6: Put **0** in the quotient. Then bring down the next digit. See if the divisor can go into the number that formed.

$$\begin{array}{r} 108\ r\ 2 \\ 36\overline{)3{,}890} \\ -\ 36\downarrow \\ \hline 290 \\ -\ 288 \\ \hline 2 \end{array}$$ ◀— 36 can go into **290**   **36 × 8 = 288**

Ted needs **108** boxes. There will be **2** zippers left over.

- You can check division with multiplication. The divisor times the quotient equals the dividend.

- Keep your columns straight when dividing. This will help you write zeros in the proper place.

B **Find each quotient.**

1. $25\overline{)5{,}030}$ **2.** $37\overline{)1{,}118}$ **3.** $17\overline{)5{,}134}$ **4.** $19\overline{)7{,}620}$ **5.** $81\overline{)8{,}424}$

6. $34\overline{)6978}$ **7.** $76\overline{)7{,}828}$ **8.** $22\overline{)6{,}910}$ **9.** $38\overline{)8{,}135}$ **10.** $67\overline{)9{,}450}$

11. $45\overline{)9{,}045}$ **12.** $55\overline{)7{,}815}$ **13.** $23\overline{)4{,}767}$ **14.** $17\overline{)3{,}537}$ **15.** $74\overline{)9{,}180}$

LESSON 14   Problem Solving with Division

Word problem
sentences that describe
a math problem

A **word problem** is a group of sentences that describes a math problem. Read the sentences and then write the division problem.

Example   Brittany is in charge of refreshments for a company picnic. She needs to buy 1,250 cans of soda. The soda is sold in cases of 48 cans. How many cases should she buy?

Step 1: State the question you must answer. This is often found at the end of a word problem. The question you must answer for this problem is *How many cases of soda should Brittany buy?*

Step 2: Make a list of the information you are given.

Her company is having a picnic.
She is in charge of refreshments.
She needs to buy 1,250 cans of soda.
A case of soda holds 48 cans.

Step 3: Make a plan to solve the problem.

1. Divide the number of cans she needs by the number of cans in one case.
2. If there is a remainder, add 1 to the quotient. Brittany will need to buy another case to have 1,250 cans.

Step 4: Follow your plan.

$$
\begin{array}{r}
26 \text{ r } 2 \\
48\overline{)1{,}250} \\
-\ 96 \\
\hline
290 \\
-\ 288 \\
\hline
2
\end{array}
$$

Brittany needs to buy **27** cases.

 Use the steps to solve each word problem.

Ross drove 464 miles to visit his sister. The trip took Ross 8 hours. How many miles did he average per hour?

1. State the question you must answer.

   _____

   _____

2. List what you know.

   _____

   _____

3. Make a plan to solve the problem.

   _____

   _____

4. Follow your plan.

Brenna paid $1,380.00 for car insurance last year.
How much did she pay each month?

5. State the question you must answer.

   _____

   _____

6. List what you know.

   _____

   _____

7. Make a plan to solve the problem.

   _____

   _____

8. Follow your plan.

B Use the same steps to solve these problems.

1. During a canned food drive, students collected 5,256 cans of food. They packed the cans in boxes of 24 cans. How many boxes did the students use?

2. Sue typed a report made up of 8,640 words. It took her two hours to type the report. How many words did Sue type per minute?

LESSON 15   Finding the Average

KEY WORDS

Average
the number found by dividing the sum of two or more quantities by the number of quantities

The **average** of a set of numbers is found by adding and then dividing. First, the set of numbers is added. Then the sum is divided by the total of numbers added.

Example   Rose scored 86, 92, 78, 85, and 94 on her first five math tests. What is Rose's average grade?

Step 1: Add the five test scores.

```
    2
   86
   92
   78
   85
 + 94
  ___
  435
```

Step 2: Divide the sum by the number of test scores.

```
        87
     5)435
     - 40
      ____
       35
     - 35
      ____
        0
```

Rose's average grade is **87**.

A   **Find the average of each set of numbers.**

1. 112, 98, 115, 91   Average _____

2. 47, 38, 55, 61, 49   Average _____

3. 28, 44, 33, 25, 51, 29 Average _____

4. 215, 237, 204, 256   Average _____

5. 98, 100, 93, 78, 85, 80 Average _____

Matt bowled 5 games in a tournament. His scores were 197, 156, 203, 184, and 173. What was his average score?

Step 1: Add the five scores.

```
   32
  197
  156
  203
  184
+ 173
 ————
  913
```

Step 2: Divide the sum by the number of scores.

$$\begin{array}{r} 182 \text{ r } 3 \quad \text{or } 182\tfrac{3}{5} \\ 5)\overline{913} \\ -\,5 \\ \hline 41 \\ -\,40 \\ \hline 13 \\ -\,10 \\ \hline 3 \end{array}$$

└─ You can show the remainder as a fraction.
Write the remainder over the divisor.

Matt's average score is **$182\tfrac{3}{5}$**.

B The table shows a bowling team's scores.
Find each bowler's average score.

	Team Member	Game 1	Game 2	Game 3	Average Score
1.	Eva	116	135	127	
2.	Rico	166	149	158	
3.	Mel	183	172	191	
4.	Dixie	154	201	165	
5.	Ben	156	171	213	

LESSON 16   Estimation

KEY WORDS

Estimate
an answer that is close
to the exact answer

People do not always need an exact answer. They want an answer that is *close to* or *about* the same as the answer. An answer that is close to the exact answer is called an **estimate.** An estimate can be made without counting. Rounding is a good way to estimate an answer.

Example   Mickey had $781.00 in his bank account. He took $84.00 out of the account to buy some clothes. About how much is left in his account?

Step 1: Round the amount of money Mickey had in the account and the amount of money he took out.

781 ⟶ 800   Round each number to the
84 ⟶ 100   nearest hundreds place.

Step 2: Find the difference between the rounded numbers.

```
  800
 −100
  ───
  700
```

Mickey has about **$700.00** in his account.

 Round to the nearest hundred to estimate the sum or difference.

1. 921 + 385   Estimate _____

2. 642 − 392   Estimate _____

3. 769 + 54   Estimate _____

4. 975 − 584   Estimate _____

5. 467 + 853   Estimate _____

6. 7,321 − 4,605   Estimate _____

7. 2,633 + 4,154   Estimate _____

8. 8,819 − 2,674   Estimate _____

9. 57,029 + 6,275   Estimate _____

10. 48,306 − 3,981   Estimate _____

When rounding,

■ find the place you are rounding to.

■ look at the digit to its right.

■ if the digit to its right is 5 or more, add one to the place you are rounding to.

■ if the digit is less than 5, do not add anything.

■ change all of the digits to the right of the place to which you are rounding to zeros.

Example   There are 54 cases of oranges on a truck. Each case holds 48 oranges. About how many oranges are on the truck?

Step 1: Round the number of cases and number of oranges in each case.

$$54 \longrightarrow 50$$
$$48 \longrightarrow 50$$

Step 2: Find the product of the rounded numbers.

$$
\begin{array}{r}
50 \\
\times\ 50 \\
\hline
00 \\
2500 \\
\hline
2500
\end{array}
$$

There are about **2,500** oranges on the truck.

B Round to the nearest ten or hundred to estimate the product or quotient.

1. 78 × 32   Estimate _____

2. 692 ÷ 109   Estimate _____

3. 44 × 59   Estimate _____

4. 915 ÷ 87   Estimate _____

5. 87 × 41   Estimate _____

6. 337 ÷ 52   Estimate _____

7. 614 × 22   Estimate _____

8. 819 ÷ 36   Estimate _____

9. 946 × 77   Estimate _____

10. 586 ÷ 29   Estimate _____

LESSON 17   Exponents

KEY WORDS

Exponent
a number that tells how many times another number is used as a factor

Base
the number that is used as a factor

An **exponent** tells how many times the same number is multiplied by itself. Exponents make math problems easier to write. The number that is to be multiplied is called the **base**. An exponent is written as a small number above the line.

| **Example** | What is the value of 5^3? |

Base $\underline{\quad}$ $\underline{\quad}$ Exponent

Step 1: Write a multiplication problem with the base used as a factor as many times as the exponent states.

$$5^3 \longrightarrow 5 \times 5 \times 5 =$$

Step 2: Find the product.

$$5 \times 5 \times 5 = 125$$

The value of 5^3 is **125**.

A Name each base and exponent.

1. 4^2 Base _____   Exponent _____

2. 8^3 Base _____   Exponent _____

3. 10^5 Base _____   Exponent _____

4. 5^4 Base _____   Exponent _____

5. 2^7 Base _____   Exponent _____

6. 7^3 Base _____   Exponent _____

7. 9^2 Base _____   Exponent _____

8. 3^4 Base _____   Exponent _____

9. 10^6 Base _____   Exponent _____

10. 2^5 Base _____   Exponent _____

Write each base and exponent as a multiplication problem.
Then find the product.

11. 3^5 _____

12. 10^4 _____

13. 2^6 _____

14. 4^3 _____

15. 5^4 _____

Example | Write $6 \times 6 \times 6 \times 6$ as a base and exponent.

Step 1: Write the base, or number used as a factor, first.

6

Step 2: Count how many times the base is multiplied. Write this number as an exponent.

6^4 An exponent is written as a small number above the line.

B Write each multiplication problem as a base and exponent.

1. $5 \times 5 \times 5 \times 5 \times 5$ _____

2. $7 \times 7 \times 7$ _____

3. $2 \times 2 \times 2 \times 2 \times 2 \times 2$ _____

4. $3 \times 3 \times 3 \times 3$ _____

5. $8 \times 8 \times 8 \times 8$ _____

6. 12×12 _____

7. $10 \times 10 \times 10 \times 10 \times 10$ _____

8. $6 \times 6 \times 6 \times 6 \times 6$ _____

9. $4 \times 4 \times 4 \times 4 \times 4$ _____

10. $1 \times 1 \times 1 \times 1 \times 1 \times 1$ _____

LESSON 18 Order of Operations

Order of operations
correct way to
complete a number
statement that has
several operations

When there are several operations in the same number statement, the **order of operations** is important. The order to use is:

Find the value of numbers with exponents.

Multiply and divide from left to right.

Add and subtract from left to right.

Example What is the value of $3^2 + 6 \times 5$?

Step 1: Find the value of any numbers with exponents.

$3^2 + 6 \times 5 \longrightarrow 9 + 6 \times 5$

Step 2: Multiply and divide from left to right.

$9 + 6 \times 5 \longrightarrow 9 + 30$

Step 3: Add and subtract from left to right.

$9 + 30 = 39$

The value of the number statement is **39**.

A Fill in the blanks to find the value of the number statement.

1. $10^2 + 6 \times 4$

___ $+ 6 \times 4$

___ $+$ ___

___

2. $72 \div 3^2 + 11$

$72 \div$ ___ $+ 11$

___ $+ 11$

___

3. $4 \times 3^3 - 8$

$4 \times$ ___ $- 8$

___ $- 8$

___

4. $5^3 - 4^2 \times 3$

___ $-$ ___ $\times 3$

___ $-$ ___

___

5. $48 \div 2^3 + 12$

$48 \div$ ___ $+ 12$

___ $+$ ___

___

6. $9^2 - 3^2 + 4 \times 3$

___ $-$ ___ $+ 4 \times 3$

___ $+$ ___

___

B Use the order of operation to find the value of each number statement.

RULES TO REMEMBER

■ Follow the order of operations one step at a time.

■ After you complete a step, write the result in the number statement.

1. $50 \div 2 - 4^2$

$50 \div 2 - \underline{}$

$\underline{} - \underline{}$

$\underline{}$

2. $8 \times 6 + 2^3 - 42 \div 7$

$8 \times 6 + \underline{} - 42 \div 7$

$\underline{} + \underline{} - \underline{}$

$\underline{}$

3. $13 \times 8 + 3^3$

$13 \times 8 + \underline{}$

$\underline{} + \underline{}$

$\underline{}$

4. $24 \times 3 - 16 \div 2^3$

$24 \times 3 - 16 \div \underline{}$

$\underline{} - \underline{}$

$\underline{}$

5. $8 + 9 \times 2^2 + 10^2 \div 5^2$

$8 + 9 \times \underline{} + \underline{} \div \underline{}$

$8 + \underline{} + \underline{}$

$\underline{}$

6. $6 \times 17 - 8^2 + 5$

$6 \times 17 - \underline{} + 5$

$\underline{} - \underline{} + 5$

$\underline{}$

7. $7 \times 9 \div 3 + 4^2$

$7 \times 9 \div 3 + \underline{}$

$\underline{} + \underline{}$

$\underline{}$

8. $10^3 - 5^3 \times 2^2$

$\underline{} - \underline{} \times \underline{}$

$\underline{} - \underline{}$

$\underline{}$

LESSON 19   Common Factors

KEY WORDS

Common factors
for any two numbers,
all the numbers that
divide evenly into
both numbers

**Greatest
common factor**
the largest factor
of two numbers

The numbers that divide evenly into a number are the number's factors. Factors that divide evenly into two numbers are **common factors.**

Example   What are the common factors of 12 and 15?

Step 1: List all the factors of the numbers.

12	**15**
1 × 12	1 × 15
2 × 6	_____
3 × 4	3 × 5
4 × 3 ← Factors repeat,	_____
so stop here. →	5 × 3

Step 2: Underline the factors that appear in both lists.

12	**15**
1 × 12	**1** × 15
2 × 6	_____
3 × 4	**3** × 5

Step 3: List these common factors.

(1, 3)

The common factors of **12** and **15** are **1** and **3**.

A Find the common factors of each number pair.

1. 18 and 30

Common factors_____

2. 20 and 35

Common factors_____

3. 16 and 24

Common factors_____

4. 27 and 51

Common factors_____

5. 10 and 25

Common factors_____

6. 36 and 48

Common factors_____

7. 24 and 56

Common factors_____

8. 7 and 13

Common factors_____

The largest factor that divides evenly into two numbers is called the **greatest common factor.**

Example What is the greatest common factor of 14 and 42?

Step 1: List all the factors of the numbers.

14	42
1 × 14	1 × 42
2 × 7	2 × 21
	3 × 14
	6 × 7

Step 2: Underline the factors that appear in both lists.

14	42
1 × 14	1 × 42
2 × 7	2 × 21
	3 × 14
	6 × 7

Step 3: List these common factors. The largest number is the greatest common factor.

(1, 2, 7, 14)

The greatest common factor of **14** and **42** is **14**.

B Find the greatest common factor of each number pair.

1. 30 and 60

Common factors_____   Greatest common factor_____

2. 24 and 72

Common factors_____   Greatest common factor_____

3. 16 and 64

Common factors_____   Greatest common factor_____

4. 36 and 45

Common factors_____   Greatest common factor_____

5. 35 and 56

Common factors_____   Greatest common factor_____

LESSON 20   Least Common Multiple

KEY WORDS

Multiple
the product of a given number and another whole number

Least common multiple
the smallest number that two numbers will divide

The **multiples** of a number are the answers you get when you multiply the number by another whole number. The **least common multiple** is the smallest number that two numbers will divide.

Example   What is the least common multiple of 8 and 20?

Step 1: List the first few **multiples** of both numbers. To list multiples of a number, write the product of the number and 1, the number and 2, and so on.

8 ———▶ 8   16   24   32   40   48   56   64
20 ———▶ 20   40   60   80   100

Step 2: Underline the smallest nonzero number that is in both lists.

8 ———▶ 8   16   24   32   **40**   48   56   64
20 ———▶ 20   **40**   60   80   100

The least common multiple of 8 and 20 is **40.**

 A List the multiples of both numbers.
Then find the least common multiple.

1. 4 _____

6 _____

Least common multiple _____

2. 8 _____

10 _____

Least common multiple _____

3. 15 _____

20 _____

Least common multiple _____

4. 18 _____

27 _____

Least common multiple _____

5. 4 _____

16 _____

Least common multiple _____

6. 9 _____

12 _____

Least common multiple _____

7. 5 _____

6 _____

Least common multiple _____

8. 6 _____

9 _____

Least common multiple _____

9. 20 _____

25 _____

Least common multiple _____

10. 3 _____

7 _____

Least common multiple _____

B Circle the number that answers each question.

1. Which number is a common multiple of 4 and 6?

8   12   18

2. Which number is not a common multiple of 4 and 6?

24   16   12

3. Which number is a common multiple of 8 and 3?

12   18   24

4. Which number is not a common multiple of 8 and 3?

24   12   48

LESSON 21   Using a Calculator

KEY WORDS

Calculator
tool used to perform
math operations

You can use a **calculator** to help you do math problems quickly and accurately. You can use it to find multiples and to check your work.

Example   How can Walt use a calculator to find the first five multiples of 14?

Step 1: Turn the calculator on. Press ON/C .

Step 2: Press + 1 4 = . The display shows 14 .
That's because 14 × 1 = 14.

Step 3: Press = . The display shows 28 .
That's because 14 × 2 = 28.

Step 4: Press = . The display shows the next multiple of 14.
Continue pressing = to find other multiples of 14.

Step 5: Record the multiples. Then press C to clear the calculator.

The first five multiples of 14 are **14, 28, 42, 56** and **70**.

A Use a calculator to find the first five multiples of each number.

1. 24 _____ _____ _____ _____ _____

2. 17 _____ _____ _____ _____ _____

3. 50 _____ _____ _____ _____ _____

4. 15 _____ _____ _____ _____ _____

5. 32 _____ _____ _____ _____ _____

6. 35 _____ _____ _____ _____ _____

7. 19 _____ _____ _____ _____ _____

8. 25 _____ _____ _____ _____ _____

9. 100 _____ _____ _____ _____ _____

10. 21 _____ _____ _____ _____ _____

Example Jen divided 200 by 18. She said the quotient is 11 r 2. How can Jen use a calculator to check her work?

Step 1: Turn the calculator on. Press ON/C

Step 2: Press 1 8 × 1 1 = The display shows 198. That's because 18 × 11 = 198.

Step 3: Add the remainder. Press + 2 =. The display shows 200.

Step 4: Press C to clear the calculator.

Jen's answer is correct.

B Use a calculator to check each division problem. If the work is correct, write Correct on the line. If the work is incorrect, write the correct answer on the line.

1. $354 \div 15 = 23$ r 9 _____

2. $782 \div 25 = 31$ r 10 _____

3. $529 \div 37 = 14$ r 10 _____

4. $416 \div 18 = 23$ r 2 _____

5. $757 \div 13 = 58$ r 3 _____

6. $921 \div 42 = 21$ r 39 _____

7. $187 \div 9 = 20$ r 7 _____

8. $648 \div 16 = 40$ r 4 _____

9. $1,540 \div 65 = 23$ r 45 _____

10. $7,982 \div 22 = 362$ r 20 _____

UNIT TEST

Part 1
Matching Definitions

Match each word in Column A with its definition in Column B.

Column A	Column B
_____ **1.** Addend	**A.** answer to a multiplication problem
_____ **2.** Remainder	**B.** answer to a subtraction problem
_____ **3.** Dividend	**C.** answer to an addition problem
_____ **4.** Difference	**D.** to write a number as groups of ones and tens
_____ **5.** Factors	**E.** number being added to another number
_____ **6.** Product	**F.** renaming a number as a simpler number
_____ **7.** Quotient	**G.** number being split into equal groups
_____ **8.** Rename	**H.** amount left over when dividing
_____ **9.** Rounding	**I.** answer to a division problem
_____ **10.** Sum	**J.** numbers that are multiplied

Part 2
Place Values

Write the name of the place value for each underlined digit.

1. 45,**7**91,835 _____

2. **8**5,609,124 _____

3. 179,04**3**,646 _____

Part 3
Rounding Numbers

Round each number to the place named.

1. 17,905 (thousands)_____

2. 4,572,885 (hundreds) _____

3. 852,408,153 (millions)_____

Part 4
Addition

Find the sum.

1. 665
    + 214

2. 713
    + 186

3. 4,872
    + 3,145

4. 549
    + 870

5. 3,001
    + 4,569

Part 5
Subtraction

Subtract.

1. 4,876
    − 1,523

2. 735
    − 95

3. 2,143
    − 1,542

4. 949
    − 367

5. 5,000
    − 3,768

Part 6
Multiplication

Multiply.

1. 56
    × 27

2. 175
    × 31

3. 492
    × 65

4. 816
    × 73

5. 387
    × 59

Part 7
Division

Divide.

1. $16\overline{)304}$

2. $28\overline{)364}$

3. $31\overline{)190}$

4. $47\overline{)1,180}$

5. $53\overline{)1,544}$

Part 8
Word Problems

Solve each word problem.

1. Ali worked 37 hours last week. She earns $6.85 an hour. How much did Ali earn last week?

2. Students at Oak Crest High School collected 1,010 cans of food. They are packing the cans in boxes. Each box can hold 36 cans. How many boxes do the students need to pack all the cans?

3. Wilson High School has 517 ninth grade students, 642 tenth grade students, 479 eleventh grade students, and 411 twelfth grade students. Altogether, how many students attend Wilson High School?

Part 9
Find the Value

Find the value of each exponent.

1. 5^4 _____

2. 3^5 _____

Part 10
Common Factors, and Multiples

Find each common factor or multiple.

1. What are three common factors of 14 and 42? _____

2. What is the greatest common factor of 12 and 30? _____

3. What is the least common multiple of 18 and 24? _____

LESSON 22   What Is a Fraction?

KEY WORDS

Fraction
part of a whole number

Numerator
the top number of a fraction that tells how many parts are used

Denominator
the bottom number of a fraction that tells the number of parts to the whole

A **fraction** is a number that names part of a whole. A fraction has a **numerator** and a **denominator**. The numerator tells how many parts are used. The denominator tells how many parts in the whole.

Example What fraction shows how many parts of the figure are shaded?

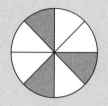

Step 1: Count the number of shaded parts in the figure. Write the number.

3

Step 2: Draw a line under the number. This is the fraction bar.

$\underline{3}$

Step 3: Count the number of parts in the whole figure. Write the number under the fraction bar.

$\frac{3}{8}$ ← numerator
  ← denominator

$\frac{3}{8}$ of the figure is shaded

A Write a fraction to show how many parts of each figure are shaded. Then write another fraction to show how many parts are not shaded.

1.
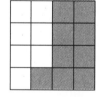

Shaded _____
Not shaded _____

2.
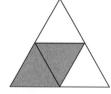

Shaded _____
Not shaded _____

3.

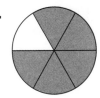

Shaded _____
Not shaded _____

4.

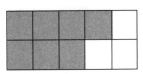

Shaded _____
Not shaded _____

5.

Shaded _____
Not shaded _____

6.

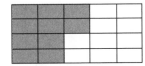

Shaded _____
Not shaded _____

7.

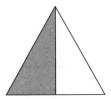

Shaded _____
Not shaded _____

8.

Shaded _____
Not shaded _____

9.

Shaded _____
Not shaded _____

10.

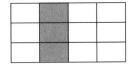

Shaded _____
Not shaded _____

LESSON 23   Comparing Fractions

KEY WORDS

Compare
to find the largest
or smallest number

Cross product
product of the
numerator of one
fraction and the
denominator of
another fraction

Like fractions
fractions that have the
same denominator

Unlike fractions
fractions that have
different denominators

To **compare** fractions is to find the largest and smallest fraction. **Like fractions** are fractions that have the same denominator. To compare like fractions, compare the numerator, or top number, of each fraction. The fraction with the largest numerator is the largest fraction. Use the less than sign to show which fraction is smaller.

Example Which is larger, $\frac{3}{6}$ or $\frac{5}{6}$?

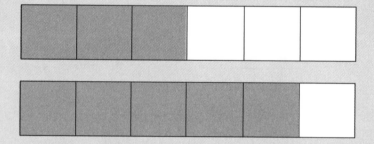

Step 1: Look at the shaded figures. 5 is larger than 3

Step 2: Use the less than < sign to show which fraction is smaller.

$$\frac{3}{6} < \frac{5}{6}$$

$\frac{5}{6}$ is less than $\frac{3}{6}$.

A Compare the fractions. Write < (is less than) or > (is greater than) on the line.

1. $\frac{2}{5}$ _____ $\frac{4}{5}$

2. $\frac{7}{9}$ _____ $\frac{4}{9}$

3. $\frac{3}{4}$ _____ $\frac{1}{4}$

4. $\frac{7}{8}$ _____ $\frac{5}{8}$

5. $\frac{5}{15}$ _____ $\frac{11}{15}$

6. $\frac{3}{7}$ _____ $\frac{6}{7}$

7. $\frac{1}{3}$ _____ $\frac{2}{3}$

8. $\frac{1}{6}$ _____ $\frac{5}{6}$

Unlike fractions have different denominators. To **compare** unlike fractions, you can use **cross products**. A cross product is the product of the numerator of one fraction and the denominator of another fraction.

Example Compare $\frac{3}{5}$ and $\frac{5}{10}$.

Step 1: Find the product of the numerator of the first fraction and the denominator of the second fraction. This is the cross product. Write the cross product by the numerator.

$30 \rightarrow \frac{3}{5}$ and $\frac{5}{10}$.   The product of 3 and 10 is 30.
$3 \times 10 = 30$

Step 2: Find the product of the numerator of the second fraction and the denominator of the first fraction. Write the cross product by the numerator.

$25 \rightarrow \frac{3}{5}$ and $\frac{5}{10}$.   The product of 5 and 5 is 25.
$5 \times 5 = 25$

Step 3: Compare the cross products. Use the greater than $>$ sign to show which fraction is larger.

$30 > 25$ 30 is greater than 25

$\frac{3}{5} > \frac{5}{10}$

$\frac{3}{5}$ is greater than $\frac{5}{10}$.

B Find the cross products. Tell whether the first fraction is less than ($<$), greater than ($>$), or equal to ($=$) the second fraction.

1. $\frac{3}{7}$ _____ $\frac{2}{3}$

2. $\frac{5}{10}$ _____ $\frac{1}{2}$

3. $\frac{54}{55}$ _____ $\frac{5}{9}$

4. $\frac{7}{16}$ _____ $\frac{1}{4}$

5. $\frac{3}{6}$ _____ $\frac{5}{9}$

6. $\frac{1}{10}$ _____ $\frac{10}{100}$

7. $\frac{11}{12}$ _____ $\frac{8}{9}$

8. $\frac{3}{5}$ _____ $\frac{2}{3}$

9. $\frac{7}{30}$ _____ $\frac{7}{25}$

10. $\frac{4}{8}$ _____ $\frac{3}{4}$

11. $\frac{6}{7}$ _____ $\frac{9}{10}$

12. $\frac{16}{20}$ _____ $\frac{4}{5}$

13. $\frac{1}{5}$ _____ $\frac{5}{18}$

14. $\frac{2}{7}$ _____ $\frac{3}{14}$

LESSON 24   Renaming Fractions in Simplest Form

KEY WORDS

Simplest form
a fraction in which the numerator and denominator have no common factor greater than 1

Simplify
to express a fraction in lowest terms

When you are doing fraction problems, the answer often needs to be **simplified**, or renamed, in the lowest terms. To simplify a fraction, divide the numerator and the denominator by the largest number that divides into both evenly. This is called the **simplest form** of the fraction. It does not change the value of the fraction.

Example Rename $\frac{9}{12}$ in simplest form.

The diagram shows that $\frac{9}{12}$ of the circle is the same as $\frac{3}{4}$ of the circle.

 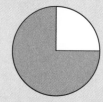

Step 1: Find the greatest common factor of 9 and 12.

Factors of 9: 1, **3**, 9

Factors of 12: 1, 2, **3**, 4, 6, 12

3 is the largest number in both lists

Step 2: Divide the numerator and denominator by 3.

$$\frac{9}{12} = \frac{9 \div 3}{12 \div 3} = \frac{3}{4} \longleftarrow \quad \frac{3}{4} \text{ is the simplest form of } \frac{9}{12}$$

A **Find the greatest common factor.**
Rename each fraction in simplest form.

1. $\frac{16}{20}$

Factors of 16 _____

Factors of 20 _____

Greatest common factor _____

Simplest form _____

2. $\frac{7}{28}$

Factors of 7 _____

Factors of 28 _____

Greatest common factor _____

Simplest form _____

3. $\frac{9}{18}$

Factors of 9 _____

Factors of 18 _____

Greatest common factor _____

Simplest form _____

4. $\frac{10}{50}$

Factors of 10 _____

Factors of 50 _____

Greatest common factor _____

Simplest form _____

B Rename each fraction in simplest form.

1. $\frac{12}{18}$ _____

2. $\frac{25}{35}$ _____

3. $\frac{6}{9}$ _____

4. $\frac{27}{54}$ _____

5. $\frac{33}{77}$ _____

6. $\frac{46}{50}$ _____

7. $\frac{2}{100}$ _____

8. $\frac{14}{21}$ _____

9. $\frac{24}{36}$ _____

10. $\frac{56}{64}$ _____

11. $\frac{12}{30}$ _____

12. $\frac{9}{11}$ _____

13. $\frac{26}{40}$ _____

14. $\frac{45}{60}$ _____

15. $\frac{10}{55}$ _____

16. $\frac{16}{32}$ _____

17. $\frac{36}{45}$ _____

18. $\frac{50}{75}$ _____

19. $\frac{21}{56}$ _____

20. $\frac{18}{30}$ _____

LESSON 25   Improper Fractions

Improper fraction
a fraction with a numerator that is equal to or larger than the denominator

Mixed number
a number made up of a whole number and a fraction

Whole number
numbers such as 0, 1, 2, 3, 4, 5

An **improper fraction** is a fraction where the numerator is equal to or greater than the denominator. A **mixed number** is made up of a **whole number** and a fraction. An improper fraction can be renamed as a mixed number by dividing the numerator by the denominator. If the denominator is a factor of the numerator, the improper fraction will become a whole number.

Example Rename $\frac{30}{7}$ as a mixed number.

Step 1: Divide the numerator by the denominator.

$$
\begin{array}{r}
4 \text{ r } 2 \\
7\overline{)30} \\
-28 \\
\hline
2
\end{array}
$$

Step 2: Write the answer as a whole number and a fraction. Write the remainder over the divisor.

$$4\frac{2}{7} \longleftarrow \begin{array}{l}\textbf{numerator is the remainder} \\ \textbf{denominator is the divisor}\end{array}$$

Example Rename $\frac{32}{8}$

Step 1: Divide the numerator by the denominator.

$$
\begin{array}{r}
4 \\
8\overline{)32} \\
-32 \\
\hline
0
\end{array}
$$

Step 2: When there is no remainder, write the answer as a whole number.

$\frac{32}{8}$ is renamed as **4**.

Rename each improper fraction as a mixed number.

1. $\frac{17}{5}$ _____

2. $\frac{9}{2}$ _____

3. $\frac{29}{8}$ _____

4. $\frac{30}{5}$ _____

5. $\frac{43}{8}$ _____

6. $\frac{38}{9}$ _____

7. $\frac{8}{5}$ _____

8. $\frac{24}{6}$ _____

9. $\frac{71}{10}$ _____

10. $\frac{33}{5}$ _____

11. $\frac{65}{7}$ _____

12. $\frac{35}{7}$ _____

13. $\frac{29}{4}$ _____

14. $\frac{43}{9}$ _____

15. $\frac{42}{6}$ _____

16. $\frac{18}{3}$ _____

17. $\frac{51}{25}$ _____

18. $\frac{17}{3}$ _____

19. $\frac{12}{5}$ _____

20. $\frac{27}{9}$ _____

21. $\frac{73}{7}$ _____

22. $\frac{95}{5}$ _____

23. $\frac{109}{10}$ _____

24. $\frac{61}{8}$ _____

RULES TO REMEMBER

■ If the denominator is a factor of the numerator, the improper fraction will become a whole number.

LESSON 26   Writing Mixed Numbers in Simplest Form

KEY WORDS

Mixed number
a number made up of a whole number and a fraction

Simplest form
a fraction with a numerator and denominator that have no common factor greater than 1

Often the answer to a fraction problem will be a **mixed number** that is not in its **simplest form**. The mixed number needs to be renamed as a whole number, and the fraction needs to be renamed in simplest form.

Example   Rename $4\frac{6}{15}$ in simplest form.

Step 1: Find the greatest common factor of 6 and 15.

Factors of 6:   1, 2, **3**, 6   **3** is the largest number in both lists

Factors of 15: 1, **3**, 5, 15

Step 2: Divide the numerator and denominator by 3.

$$4\frac{6}{15} = 4\frac{6 \div 3}{15 \div 3} = 4\frac{2}{5} \longleftarrow \quad 4\frac{2}{5} \text{ is the simplest form of } 4\frac{6}{15}.$$

 A Rename each mixed number in simplest form.

1. $5\frac{7}{21}$ _____   7. $12\frac{8}{72}$ _____

2. $3\frac{9}{36}$ _____   8. $6\frac{14}{28}$ _____

3. $7\frac{12}{20}$ _____   9. $5\frac{15}{18}$ _____

4. $8\frac{33}{55}$ _____   10. $1\frac{6}{8}$ _____

5. $3\frac{35}{50}$ _____   11. $3\frac{8}{24}$ _____

6. $2\frac{4}{18}$ _____   12. $9\frac{7}{35}$ _____

Sometimes the mixed number will include an improper fraction. Then the improper fraction needs to be changed to a mixed number and added to the whole number.

Example | Rename $2\frac{9}{4}$ in simplest form.

Step 1: Change the improper fraction into a mixed number.

$$2\frac{9}{4} = 2 + \frac{9}{4} = 2 + 2\frac{1}{4} \longleftarrow 9 \div 4 = 2\ r\ 1$$

Step 2: Add the whole numbers.

$$2 + 2\frac{1}{4} = 4\frac{1}{4} \longleftarrow 4\frac{1}{4} \text{ is the simplest form of } 2\frac{9}{4}.$$

B Rename each mixed number in simplest form.

1. $5\frac{13}{7}$ _____

2. $3\frac{51}{25}$ _____

3. $8\frac{18}{5}$ _____

4. $4\frac{6}{2}$ _____

5. $7\frac{9}{4}$ _____

6. $9\frac{21}{10}$ _____

7. $7\frac{5}{3}$ _____

8. $10\frac{9}{6}$ _____

9. $2\frac{11}{7}$ _____

10. $6\frac{15}{8}$ _____

11. $42\frac{18}{7}$ _____

12. $14\frac{27}{12}$ _____

LESSON 27   ## Multiplying Fractions

You can multiply fractions. First multiply the numerators. Then multiply the denominators. Next you simplify the product.

Example   What is the product of $\frac{3}{4}$ and $\frac{2}{5}$?

Step 1: Multiply the numerators.

$$\frac{3}{4} \times \frac{2}{5} = 3 \times 2 = 6$$

Step 2: Multiply the denominators.

$$\frac{3}{4} \times \frac{2}{5} = \frac{3 \times 2}{4 \times 5} = \frac{6}{20}$$

Step 3: Simplify the product.

$$\frac{3}{4} \times \frac{2}{5} = \frac{3 \times 2}{4 \times 5} = \frac{6 \div 2}{20 \div 2} = \frac{3}{10}$$

The product of $\frac{3}{4}$ and $\frac{2}{5}$ is $\frac{3}{10}$.

 Multiply the fractions. Write each product in simplest form.

1. $\frac{3}{5} \times \frac{7}{8}$ _____

2. $\frac{9}{10} \times \frac{1}{2}$ _____

3. $\frac{8}{9} \times \frac{5}{6}$ _____

4. $\frac{2}{7} \times \frac{6}{10}$ _____

5. $\frac{1}{3} \times \frac{5}{6}$ _____

6. $\frac{4}{5} \times \frac{8}{9}$ _____

7. $\frac{1}{6} \times \frac{3}{4}$ _____

8. $\frac{2}{9} \times \frac{4}{7}$ _____

9. $\frac{6}{11} \times \frac{3}{4}$ _____

10. $\frac{5}{6} \times \frac{2}{3}$ _____

11. $\frac{3}{4} \times \frac{1}{2}$ _____

12. $\frac{1}{8} \times \frac{6}{9}$ _____

Sometimes you can simplify the problem before multiplying. See if the numerators and the denominators have any common factors. If they do, divide both the numerators and denominators by their common factor. Then multiply.

Example | What is the product of $\frac{5}{8}$ and $\frac{4}{10}$?

Step 1: 5 and 10 have a common factor, 5. Divide 5 and 10 by 5.

$$\frac{\overset{1}{\cancel{5}}}{8} \times \frac{4}{\underset{2}{\cancel{10}}}$$

Step 2: 8 and 4 have a common factor, 4. Divide 8 and 4 by 4.

$$\frac{\overset{1}{\cancel{5}}}{\underset{2}{\cancel{8}}} \times \frac{\overset{1}{\cancel{4}}}{\underset{2}{\cancel{10}}}$$

Step 3: Multiply the numerators. Multiply the denominators.

$$\frac{\overset{1}{\cancel{5}}}{\underset{2}{\cancel{8}}} \times \frac{\overset{1}{\cancel{4}}}{\underset{2}{\cancel{10}}} = \frac{1 \times 1}{2 \times 2} = \frac{1}{4}$$

The product of $\frac{5}{8}$ and $\frac{4}{10}$ is $\frac{1}{4}$.

B **Simplify the problems first, then multiply the fractions.**

1. $\frac{5}{6} \times \frac{3}{15}$ _____

2. $\frac{9}{8} \times \frac{2}{3}$ _____

3. $\frac{8}{9} \times \frac{3}{6}$ _____

4. $\frac{2}{7} \times \frac{14}{20}$ _____

5. $\frac{9}{10} \times \frac{5}{6}$ _____

6. $\frac{4}{5} \times \frac{10}{16}$ _____

7. $\frac{1}{6} \times \frac{3}{4}$ _____

8. $\frac{2}{9} \times \frac{6}{8}$ _____

9. $\frac{6}{7} \times \frac{1}{12}$ _____

10. $\frac{4}{6} \times \frac{3}{4}$ _____

11. $\frac{3}{4} \times \frac{16}{18}$ _____

12. $\frac{7}{8} \times \frac{4}{7}$ _____

LESSON 28 Multiplying Mixed Numbers

KEY WORDS

Mixed number
a number made up of a whole number and a fraction

Improper fraction
a fraction with a numerator that is equal to or larger than the denominator

Mixed numbers must be changed to **improper fractions** before they can be multiplied. Then the numerators and denominators are multiplied. The answers are written in simplest form.

Example What is the product of $5\frac{1}{4}$ and $2\frac{2}{3}$?

Step 1: Rename the mixed numbers as improper fractions. Multiply the denominator of the fraction by the whole number. Then add the numerator to the product.

$$4 \times 5 = 20 + 1 = \frac{21}{4}$$

$$3 \times 2 = 6 + 2 = \frac{8}{3}$$

$$5\frac{1}{4} = \frac{21}{4} \qquad 2\frac{2}{3} = \frac{8}{3}$$

Step 2: Find the common factors and simplify. 21 and 3 have a common factor, 3. 4 and 8 have a common factor, 4.

$$\overset{7}{\underset{1}{\cancel{\frac{21}{4}}}} \times \overset{2}{\underset{1}{\cancel{\frac{8}{3}}}}$$

Step 3: Multiply the numerators. Multiply the denominators.

$$\overset{7}{\underset{1}{\cancel{\frac{21}{4}}}} \times \overset{2}{\underset{1}{\cancel{\frac{8}{3}}}} = \frac{14}{1} = 14$$

The product of $5\frac{1}{4}$ and $2\frac{2}{3}$ is **14**.

A Rename the mixed numbers as improper fractions. Write each product in simplest form.

1. $3\frac{3}{5} \times 1\frac{1}{6}$ _____

2. $2\frac{1}{10} \times 1\frac{2}{3}$ _____

3. $4\frac{3}{8} \times 3\frac{1}{5}$ _____

4. $1\frac{2}{7} \times 2\frac{1}{3}$ _____

5. $9\frac{1}{2} \times 1\frac{1}{3}$ _____

6. $5\frac{5}{6} \times 1\frac{4}{5}$ _____

7. $3\frac{3}{4} \times 2\frac{2}{5}$ _____

8. $1\frac{7}{8} \times 3\frac{1}{3}$ _____

9. $5\frac{1}{5} \times 3\frac{1}{8}$ _____

10. $4\frac{9}{10} \times 1\frac{3}{7}$ _____

11. $5\frac{1}{3} \times 2\frac{1}{2}$ _____

12. $4\frac{3}{8} \times 2\frac{3}{7}$ _____

To multiply fractions and whole numbers, first change the whole number to an improper fraction. The denominator of a whole number is the number 1. Then multiply the numerators. Next, multiply the denominators.

Example | What is the product of 6 and $1\frac{1}{3}$?

Step 1: Rename factors as improper fractions. Write the whole number as the numerator and 1 as the denominator.

$$6 = \frac{6}{1} \qquad 1\frac{1}{3} = \frac{4}{3}$$

Step 2: Find the common factors and simplify the fractions. 6 and 3 have a common factor, 3.

$$\frac{\overset{2}{\cancel{6}}}{1} \times \frac{4}{\underset{1}{\cancel{3}}}$$

Step 3: Multiply the numerators. Multiply the denominators.

$$\frac{\overset{2}{\cancel{6}}}{1} \times \frac{4}{\underset{1}{\cancel{3}}} = \frac{8}{1} = 8$$

The product of 6 and $1\frac{1}{3}$ is **8**.

B Rename the fractions as improper fractions. Write each product in simplest form.

1. $7\frac{1}{2} \times 1\frac{2}{3}$ _____

2. $5 \times \frac{2}{5}$ _____

3. $1\frac{7}{10} \times \frac{2}{7}$ _____

4. $3\frac{1}{3} \times 6$ _____

5. $3\frac{4}{5} \times 20$ _____

6. $5\frac{1}{6} \times 12$ _____

7. $21 \times 1\frac{2}{7}$ _____

8. $16 \times 3\frac{1}{8}$ _____

9. $9 \times \frac{3}{5}$ _____

10. $5 \times 2\frac{1}{3}$ _____

11. $1\frac{1}{2} \times 2\frac{3}{4}$ _____

12. $5\frac{2}{7} \times 3\frac{2}{7}$ _____

LESSON 29 Dilating Fractions

LESSON 29 **Dividing Fractions**

KEY WORDS

Invert
to change positions

Divisor
the number by which
you are dividing

To divide fractions, change the division sign to a multiplication sign. Then **invert** the **divisor** and multiply. To invert a fraction, the numerator and denominator change places.

Example $\frac{3}{4} \div \frac{1}{12}$

Step 1: Change the $\div$ to $\times$. Invert the divisor, or second fraction.

$$\frac{3}{4} \div \frac{1}{12} = \frac{3}{4} \times \frac{12}{1}$$

Step 2: Find the common factors and simplify.
4 and 12 have a common factor, 4.

$$_1\frac{3}{\cancel{4}} \times \frac{\cancel{12}}{1}\,^3$$

Step 3: Multiply the numerators. Multiply the denominators.

$$_1\frac{3}{\cancel{4}} \times \frac{\cancel{12}}{1}\,^3 = \frac{9}{1} = 9$$

$$\frac{3}{4} \div \frac{1}{12} = 9$$

 Divide. Write your answers in simplest form.

1. $\frac{8}{9} \div \frac{2}{3}$ _____

2. $\frac{7}{10} \div \frac{4}{5}$ _____

3. $\frac{5}{8} \div \frac{15}{16}$ _____

4. $\frac{14}{18} \div \frac{7}{9}$ _____

5. $\frac{5}{6} \div \frac{2}{3}$ _____

6. $\frac{2}{3} \div \frac{4}{15}$ _____

7. $8 \div \frac{1}{3}$ _____

8. $\frac{4}{5} \div \frac{1}{10}$ _____

9. $\frac{7}{15} \div \frac{2}{5}$ _____

10. $\frac{13}{24} \div \frac{3}{8}$ _____

11. $\frac{7}{9} \div 14$ _____

12. $\frac{6}{11} \div 2$ _____

To divide fractions and whole numbers, change the division sign to a multiplication sign. Write the whole number as a numerator with 1 as the denominator. Then invert the divisor, or second fraction. Multiply the numerators and the denominators.

RULES TO REMEMBER

■ When renaming a whole number as an improper fraction, write the whole number as the numerator and 1 as the denominator.

■ If the product is an improper fraction, rename it as a mixed number.

Example $\frac{1}{2} \div 6$

Step 1: Change the $\div$ to $\times$. Write the whole number as an improper fraction.

$$\frac{1}{2} \times 6 \qquad \frac{1}{2} \times \frac{6}{1}$$

Step 2: Invert the divisor.

$$\frac{1}{2} \times \frac{1}{6}$$

Step 3: Multiply the numerators. Multiply the denominators

$$\frac{1}{2} \times \frac{1}{6} = \frac{1}{12}$$

$$\frac{1}{2} \div 6 = \frac{1}{12}.$$

B Divide. Write your answers in simplest form.

1. $\frac{5}{6} \div 3$ _____

2. $10 \div \frac{5}{6}$ _____

3. $2 \div \frac{1}{4}$ _____

4. $2 \div \frac{1}{10}$ _____

5. $24 \div \frac{3}{4}$ _____

6. $5 \div \frac{2}{3}$ _____

7. $\frac{3}{8} \div 2$ _____

8. $6 \div \frac{1}{5}$ _____

9. $\frac{7}{10} \div 6$ _____

10. $\frac{3}{4} \div 5$ _____

11. $6 \div \frac{3}{4}$ _____

12. $3 \div \frac{1}{4}$ _____

LESSON 30   Dividing Mixed Numbers

Sometimes you need to divide a mixed number by another mixed number. First you must rename each mixed number as an improper fraction. Change the division sign to a multiplication sign. Then invert the divisor and multiply.

Example $4\frac{1}{6} \div 1\frac{2}{3}$

Step 1: Rename the mixed numbers as improper fractions.

$$4\frac{1}{6} = \frac{25}{6} \qquad 1\frac{2}{3} = \frac{5}{3}$$

Step 2: Change the ÷ to ×. Invert the divisor or second fraction.

$$\frac{25}{6} \div \frac{5}{3} = \qquad \frac{25}{6} \times \frac{3}{5}$$

Step 3: Find the common factors and simplify. 25 and 5 have a common factor, 5. 6 and 3 have a common factor, 3.

$$\overset{5}{\underset{2}{\cancel{\frac{25}{6}}}} \times \overset{1}{\underset{1}{\cancel{\frac{3}{5}}}}$$

Step 4: Multiply the numerators. Multiply the denominators. Write the product in simplest form.

$$\overset{5}{\underset{2}{\cancel{\frac{25}{6}}}} \times \overset{1}{\underset{1}{\cancel{\frac{3}{5}}}} = \frac{5}{2} = 2\frac{1}{2}$$

$$4\frac{1}{6} \div 1\frac{2}{3} = 2\frac{1}{2}$$

 Divide. Write your answers in simplest form.

1. $4\frac{1}{2} \div 1\frac{4}{5}$ _____

2. $3\frac{2}{3} \div 2\frac{1}{5}$ _____

3. $1\frac{1}{8} \div \frac{3}{16}$ _____

4. $5\frac{1}{7} \div 2\frac{1}{4}$ _____

5. $6\frac{2}{3} \div 1\frac{1}{3}$ _____

6. $5\frac{2}{5} \div 2\frac{1}{5}$ _____

7. $7\frac{1}{2} \div 1\frac{3}{7}$ _____

8. $3\frac{1}{8} \div \frac{1}{4}$ _____

To divide a mixed number by a whole number, both the mixed number and the whole number must be renamed as improper fractions. Write the whole number as a fraction with 1 as the denominator. Then invert the divisor and multiply.

9. $7\frac{1}{3} \div \frac{2}{3}$ _____

10. $5\frac{5}{6} \div 2\frac{1}{3}$ _____

11. $12 \div 4\frac{2}{7}$ _____

12. $9\frac{3}{4} \div 1\frac{5}{8}$ _____

13. $11 \div 1\frac{1}{10}$ _____

14. $3\frac{5}{6} \div 1\frac{2}{3}$ _____

15. $2\frac{3}{4} \div \frac{11}{16}$ _____

16. $20 \div 2\frac{1}{2}$ _____

17. $1\frac{1}{8} \div 4$ _____

18. $4\frac{1}{2} \div 1\frac{1}{2}$ _____

19. $\frac{9}{10} \div 1\frac{4}{5}$ _____

20. $10 \div 1\frac{3}{5}$ _____

21. $3\frac{1}{4} \div 1\frac{1}{4}$ _____

22. $2\frac{3}{5} \div \frac{1}{10}$ _____

23. $1\frac{4}{10} \div 1\frac{2}{5}$ _____

24. $8 \div \frac{4}{5}$ _____

25. $15 \div \frac{2}{3}$ _____

LESSON 31   Adding Fractions

Sometimes you need to add fractions. If the fractions have **like denominators,** or the same bottom number, add the numerators. Write the sum over the like denominator. Simplify if needed.

Example $\frac{7}{8} + \frac{5}{8} =$

Step 1: Add the numerators. Write the sum over the like denominator.

$$\frac{7}{8} + \frac{5}{8} = \frac{7+5}{8} = \frac{12}{8}$$

Step 2: Simplify the sum.

$$\frac{7}{8} + \frac{5}{8} = \frac{7+5}{8} = \frac{12}{8} = 1\frac{4}{8} = 1\frac{1}{2}$$

 Add. Write your answers in simplest form.

1. $\frac{13}{20} + \frac{9}{20}$ _____

2. $\frac{8}{9} + \frac{4}{9}$ _____

3. $\frac{1}{5} + \frac{4}{5}$ _____

4. $\frac{7}{10} + \frac{9}{10}$ _____

5. $\frac{3}{4} + \frac{3}{4}$ _____

6. $\frac{5}{6} + \frac{1}{6}$ _____

7. $\frac{7}{15} + \frac{11}{15}$ _____

8. $\frac{8}{11} + \frac{9}{11}$ _____

9. $\frac{6}{7} + \frac{5}{7}$ _____

10. $\frac{13}{18} + \frac{17}{18}$ _____

11. $\frac{11}{12} + \frac{1}{12}$ _____

12. $\frac{15}{16} + \frac{9}{16}$ _____

13. $\frac{7}{8} + \frac{9}{8}$ _____

14. $\frac{20}{21} + \frac{8}{21}$ _____

15. $\frac{5}{13} + \frac{9}{13}$ _____

Sometimes you need to add mixed numbers with like denominators. Add the whole numbers. Then add the fractions. Simplify if needed.

Example $4\frac{2}{3} + 2\frac{1}{3} =$

Step 1: Add the whole numbers.

$$4\frac{2}{3} + 2\frac{1}{3} = 6$$

Step 2: Add the numerators. Write the sum over the like denominator.

$$4\frac{2}{3} + 2\frac{1}{3} = 6\frac{3}{3}$$

Step 3: Simplify.

$$4\frac{2}{3} + 2\frac{1}{3} = 6\frac{3}{3} = 6 + 1 = 7$$

- If the sum is an improper fraction, you must rename it as a mixed number.

- Sometimes the sum of two mixed numbers is a whole number and an improper fraction. You must rename the improper fraction as a mixed number. Then add its whole number part to the sum of the whole numbers.

B **Add. Write your answers in simplest form.**

1. $4\frac{2}{5} + 3\frac{4}{5}$ _____

2. $6\frac{6}{7} + 2\frac{4}{7}$ _____

3. $9\frac{1}{2} + 3\frac{1}{2}$ _____

4. $6\frac{3}{4} + 8\frac{1}{4}$ _____

5. $7\frac{2}{3} + 4\frac{2}{3}$ _____

6. $11\frac{5}{6} + 2\frac{1}{6}$ _____

7. $4\frac{7}{8} + 3\frac{5}{8}$ _____

8. $1\frac{3}{10} + 6\frac{9}{10}$ _____

9. $2\frac{1}{2} + 1\frac{1}{2}$ _____

10. $8\frac{17}{20} + 4\frac{13}{20}$ _____

11. $6\frac{4}{5} + 3\frac{3}{5}$ _____

12. $8\frac{5}{6} + 1\frac{5}{6}$ _____

13. $3\frac{11}{12} + 1\frac{5}{12}$ _____

14. $8\frac{2}{9} + 5\frac{8}{9}$ _____

15. $1\frac{9}{10} + 5\frac{7}{10}$ _____

LESSON 32   Finding Common Denominators

KEY WORDS

Common denominators
fractions with the same denominator or bottom number

Least common denominator
the smallest number that will go into two denominators

Sometimes you need to add fractions with different denominators. Before you can add fractions, you must rename them so they have the same denominator. Fractions with the same denominator, or bottom number, have a **common denominator.** The **least common denominator** is the smallest number that is a multiple of two denominators.

Example $\frac{5}{6} + \frac{3}{10} =$

Step 1: List the first few multiples of each denominator. Underline the smallest multiple in both lists. The smallest multiple is the least common denominator.

$6 \longrightarrow 6 \quad 12 \quad 18 \quad 24 \quad \mathbf{30}$

$10 \longrightarrow 10 \quad 20 \quad \mathbf{30} \quad 40 \quad 50$

Step 2: Rename the first fraction. Use 30 as the new denominator.

$\frac{5}{6} = \frac{\ \ }{30}$ ⟵ Divide 30 by 6.

$\frac{5}{6} \times \frac{5}{5} = \frac{25}{30}$ ⟵ Multiply $\frac{5}{6} \times \frac{5}{5}$

Step 3: Rename the second fraction. Use 30 as the new denominator.

$\frac{3}{10} = \frac{\ \ }{30}$ ⟵ Divide 30 by 10.

$\frac{3}{10} \times \frac{3}{3} = \frac{9}{30}$ ⟵ Multiply $\frac{3}{10} \times \frac{3}{3}$

Step 4: Add the numerators. Write the sum over the common denominator. Simplify.

$\frac{5}{6} + \frac{3}{10} = \frac{25}{30} + \frac{9}{30} = \frac{34}{30} = 1\frac{4}{30} = 1\frac{2}{15}$

A Add these fractions. Write the sum in simplest form.

1. $\frac{5}{7} + \frac{3}{4}$ _____

2. $\frac{7}{9} + \frac{1}{3}$ _____

3. $\frac{9}{10} + \frac{5}{8}$ _____

4. $\frac{1}{2} + \frac{4}{11}$ _____

5. $\frac{8}{15} + \frac{7}{10}$ _____

6. $\frac{3}{4} + \frac{13}{20}$ _____

7. $\frac{5}{9} + \frac{7}{12}$ _____

8. $\frac{13}{18} + \frac{1}{6}$ _____

9. $\frac{17}{24} + \frac{1}{6}$ _____

10. $\frac{8}{15} + \frac{9}{20}$ _____

11. $\frac{3}{10} + \frac{5}{6}$ _____

12. $\frac{2}{5} + \frac{1}{3}$ _____

Sometimes you need to add mixed numbers with different denominators. Rename the fractions so they have a common denominator. Add the whole numbers. Then add the fractions. Simplify.

Example $2\frac{4}{5} + 6\frac{1}{4} =$

Step 1: List the first few multiples of each denominator. Underline the smallest multiple in both lists.

$5 \longrightarrow 5 \quad 10 \quad 15 \quad \mathbf{20} \quad 25$

$4 \longrightarrow 4 \quad 8 \quad 12 \quad 16 \quad \mathbf{20}$

Step 2: Rename the first mixed number. Use 20 as the new denominator.

$2\frac{4}{5} = 2\frac{}{20}$ ⟵ Divide 20 by 5.

$2\frac{4}{5} \times \frac{4}{4} = 2\frac{16}{20}$ ⟵ Multiply $\frac{4}{5} \times \frac{4}{4}$

Step 3: Rename the second mixed number. Use 20 as the new denominator.

$6\frac{1}{4} = 6\frac{}{20}$ ⟵ Divide 20 by 4.

$6\frac{1}{4} \times \frac{5}{5} = 6\frac{5}{20}$ ⟵ Multiply $\frac{1}{4} \times \frac{5}{5}$

Step 4: Add the whole numbers.

$2\frac{16}{20} + 6\frac{5}{20} = 8$

Step 5: Add the numerators. Write the sum over the common denominator. Simplify.

$2\frac{16}{20} + 6\frac{5}{20} = 8\frac{21}{20} = 9\frac{1}{20}$

B Add. Write your answers in simplest form.

1. $3\frac{3}{5} + 1\frac{1}{2}$ _____

2. $4\frac{1}{3} + 5\frac{5}{6}$ _____

3. $8\frac{1}{4} + 3\frac{1}{2}$ _____

4. $4\frac{6}{7} + 2\frac{1}{4}$ _____

5. $1\frac{5}{8} + 6\frac{1}{6}$ _____

6. $3\frac{2}{3} + 5\frac{3}{4}$ _____

7. $4\frac{7}{10} + 2\frac{1}{2}$ _____

8. $6\frac{5}{9} + 2\frac{5}{6}$ _____

9. $2\frac{4}{7} + 3\frac{3}{4}$ _____

10. $1\frac{7}{12} + 2\frac{3}{4}$ _____

11. $6\frac{1}{8} + 4\frac{1}{6}$ _____

12. $1\frac{9}{10} + 8\frac{4}{5}$ _____

LESSON 33 Subtracting Fractions

KEY WORDS

Common denominators
fractions with the same denominator or bottom number

Sometimes you need to subtract fractions. If the fractions have a common denominator, just subtract the numerators. Write the difference over the like denominator. Then simplify the answer.

Example $\frac{8}{9} - \frac{2}{9} =$

Step 1: Subtract the numerators. Write the difference over the like denominator.

$$\frac{8}{9} - \frac{2}{9} = \frac{8-2}{9} = \frac{6}{9}$$

Step 2: Simplify the difference.

$$\frac{8}{9} - \frac{2}{9} = \frac{8-2}{9} = \frac{6}{9} = \frac{2}{3}$$

 Subtract. Write your answers in simplest form.

1. $\frac{7}{10} - \frac{2}{10}$ _____

2. $\frac{7}{8} - \frac{3}{8}$ _____

3. $\frac{4}{5} - \frac{2}{5}$ _____

4. $\frac{6}{7} - \frac{2}{7}$ _____

5. $\frac{3}{4} - \frac{1}{4}$ _____

6. $\frac{5}{6} - \frac{3}{6}$ _____

7. $\frac{13}{15} - \frac{8}{15}$ _____

8. $\frac{11}{12} - \frac{7}{12}$ _____

9. $\frac{17}{24} - \frac{7}{24}$ _____

10. $\frac{13}{18} - \frac{4}{18}$ _____

11. $\frac{11}{21} - \frac{8}{21}$ _____

12. $\frac{9}{14} - \frac{2}{14}$ _____

Sometimes you need to subtract mixed numbers with different denominators. Rename the fractions so they have a common denominator. Find the difference between the whole numbers. Then subtract the fractions. Simplify if needed.

Example $5\frac{3}{4} - 3\frac{1}{6} =$

Step 1: List the first few multiples of each denominator. Underline the smallest multiple in both lists.

$$4 \longrightarrow 4 \quad 8 \quad \mathbf{12} \quad 16$$
$$6 \longrightarrow 6 \quad \mathbf{12} \quad 18 \quad 24$$

Step 2: Rename the first mixed number. Use 12 as the new denominator.

$$5\frac{3}{4} = 5\frac{}{12} \longleftarrow \text{Divide 12 by 4.}$$
$$5\frac{3}{4} \times \frac{3}{3} = 5\frac{9}{12} \longleftarrow \text{Multiply } \frac{3}{4} \times \frac{3}{3}$$

Step 3: Rename the second mixed number. Use 12 as the new denominator.

$$3\frac{1}{6} = 3\frac{}{12} \longleftarrow \text{Divide 12 by 6.}$$
$$3\frac{1}{6} \times \frac{2}{2} = 3\frac{2}{12} \longleftarrow \text{Multiply } \frac{1}{6} \times \frac{2}{2}$$

Step 4: Subtract the whole numbers.

$$5\frac{9}{12} - 3\frac{2}{12} = 2$$

Step 5: Subtract the numerators. Write the difference over the common denominator.

$$5\frac{9}{12} - 3\frac{2}{12} = 2\frac{7}{12}$$

B   **Subtract. Write your answers in simplest form.**

1. $8\frac{4}{5} - 5\frac{2}{3}$ _____

2. $6\frac{7}{9} - 2\frac{1}{2}$ _____

3. $9\frac{2}{3} - 5\frac{1}{4}$ _____

4. $5\frac{3}{4} - 1\frac{1}{16}$ _____

5. $7\frac{5}{6} - 4\frac{1}{2}$ _____

6. $12\frac{9}{10} - 4\frac{3}{5}$ _____

7. $2\frac{7}{8} - 1\frac{2}{3}$ _____

8. $10\frac{6}{7} - 4\frac{1}{3}$ _____

9. $5\frac{8}{9} - 4\frac{1}{6}$ _____

10. $8\frac{19}{20} - 2\frac{3}{10}$ _____

11. $3\frac{13}{15} - 2\frac{4}{5}$ _____

12. $4\frac{5}{6} - 1\frac{2}{3}$ _____

LESSON 34   Subtracting Fractions with Renaming

You can subtract a fraction from a whole number. First you rename the whole number as a mixed number with the same denominator as the fraction. Then you subtract.

Example

$$12$$
$$-\ \frac{3}{4}$$
_____

Step 1: Rename the whole number as a mixed number.

$$12 = 11\frac{4}{4}$$
$$-\ \frac{3}{4} = \ \ \frac{3}{4}$$
_____

Step 2: Subtract the whole numbers.

$$12 = 11\frac{4}{4}$$
$$-\ \frac{3}{4} = \ \ \frac{3}{4}$$
_____
$$11 \qquad\qquad 11 - 0 = 11$$

Step 3: Subtract the numerators. Write the difference over the common denominator.

$$12 = 11\frac{4}{4}$$
$$-\ \frac{3}{4} = \ \ \frac{3}{4}$$
_____
$$11\frac{1}{4} \qquad\qquad 12 - \frac{3}{4} = 11\frac{1}{4}$$

A Subtract. Write your answers in simplest form.

1. $6 - \frac{2}{7}$ _____   **4.** $12 - \frac{6}{11}$ _____   **7.** $13 - \frac{5}{8}$ _____

2. $11 - \frac{3}{8}$ _____   **5.** $8 - \frac{9}{10}$ _____   **8.** $5 - \frac{5}{6}$ _____

3. $7 - \frac{1}{6}$ _____   **6.** $7 - \frac{4}{9}$ _____   **9.** $7 - \frac{2}{3}$ _____

In some problems, renaming fractions forms a top fraction that is less than a bottom fraction. In order to find their difference, you must rename the top fraction.

RULES TO REMEMBER

■ You can only add fractions with common denominators.

■ Any fraction that has the same number as its numerator and denominator is equal to one.

Example

$$3\frac{1}{8}$$
$$-1\frac{5}{6}$$

Step 1: List the first few multiples of each denominator. Underline the smallest multiple in both lists.

8 ⟶ 8   16   **24**

6 ⟶ 6   12   18   **24**

Step 2: Rename the first mixed number. Use 24 as the new denominator.

$$3\frac{1}{8} = 3\frac{}{24} \longleftarrow \text{Divide 24 by 8.}$$
$$3\frac{1}{8} \times \frac{3}{3} = 3\frac{3}{24} \longleftarrow \text{Multiply } \frac{1}{8} \times \frac{3}{3}$$

Step 3: Rename the second mixed number. Use 24 as the new denominator.

$$1\frac{5}{6} = 1\frac{}{24} \longleftarrow \text{Divide 24 by 6.}$$
$$1\frac{5}{6} \times \frac{4}{4} = 1\frac{20}{24} \longleftarrow \text{Multiply } \frac{5}{6} \times \frac{4}{4}$$

Step 4: Rename the first fraction so its numerator is larger than the numerator of the second fraction.

$$3\frac{3}{24} = 2 + \frac{3}{24} + \frac{24}{24} = 2\frac{27}{24}$$
$$-1\frac{20}{24} \xrightarrow{\hspace{3cm}} 1\frac{20}{24}$$

Step 5: Subtract.

$$2\frac{27}{24}$$
$$-1\frac{20}{24}$$
$$\overline{1\frac{7}{24}}$$ $$3\frac{1}{8} - 1\frac{5}{6} = 1\frac{7}{24}$$

B Subtract. Write your answers in simplest form.

1. $5\frac{1}{5} - 2\frac{7}{10}$ _____

2. $6\frac{3}{7} - 4\frac{1}{2}$ _____

3. $3\frac{2}{9} - 1\frac{2}{3}$ _____

4. $11\frac{1}{4} - 7\frac{7}{8}$ _____

5. $4\frac{1}{2} - 2\frac{5}{6}$ _____

6. $9\frac{2}{15} - 3\frac{4}{5}$ _____

7. $8\frac{5}{16} - 3\frac{7}{8}$ _____

8. $4\frac{2}{7} - 1\frac{3}{4}$ _____

9. $6\frac{7}{10} - 4\frac{17}{20}$ _____

UNIT 2 *Fractions*   73

LESSON 35   Problem Solving with Fractions

A word problem is a group of sentences that describes a math problem. Read the sentences and then answer the fraction problem.

Example   Adam jogged $3\frac{1}{4}$ miles on Monday and $4\frac{1}{2}$ miles on Wednesday. His coach wants Adam to jog a total of 10 miles each week. How much farther does Adam need to jog this week?

Step 1: State the question you must answer. This is often found at the end of a word problem. The question you must answer for this problem is *How much farther does Adam need to jog?*

Step 2: Make a list of the information you are given.

He jogged $3\frac{1}{4}$ miles on Monday.

He jogged $4\frac{1}{2}$ miles on Wednesday.

His coach wants Adam to jog 10 miles each week.

Step 3: Make a plan to solve the problem.

1. Add the distances Adam jogged on Monday and Wednesday.

2. Subtract the sum from 10.

Step 4: Follow your plan.

$$3\frac{1}{4} = 3\frac{1}{4} \qquad\qquad 10 = 9\frac{4}{4} \quad \text{Rename 10 as } 9\frac{4}{4}$$
$$\underline{+\,4\frac{1}{2} = 4\frac{2}{4}} \qquad\qquad \underline{-\,7\frac{3}{4} \qquad 7\frac{3}{4}}$$
$$7\frac{3}{4} \qquad\qquad\qquad 2\frac{1}{4}$$

Adam still needs to jog **$2\frac{1}{4}$** miles.

 Use the steps to solve each word problem

Marco is working on a science project. He has $5\frac{3}{4}$ ft of wire. He will use $2\frac{7}{8}$ ft in the project. How much wire will Marco have left?

1. State the question you must answer.

_____

_____

2. List what you know.

_____

_____

3. Make a plan to solve the problem.

_____

_____

4. Follow your plan.

Kathy is baking cookies. She uses $1\frac{3}{4}$ cup of sugar and $2\frac{1}{8}$ cup of flour to make one batch. How much sugar and flour does Kathy need to make three batches?

5. State the question you must answer.

_____

_____

6. List what you know.

_____

_____

7. Make a plan to solve the problem.

_____

_____

8. Follow your plan.

B Use the same steps to solve these problems.

1. Beth has $10\frac{1}{2}$ yd of cloth. She is using the cloth to make photo albums. She needs $\frac{3}{4}$ yd of the cloth for each album. How many albums can Beth make?

2. Blair lost $\frac{7}{8}$ pound on the first week of her diet. During the second week, she lost $1\frac{2}{3}$ pounds. She lost $1\frac{1}{2}$ pounds during the third week. How much weight did Blair lose after dieting for three weeks?

UNIT TEST

Part 1
Matching Definitions

Match each word in Column A with its definition in Column B.

	Column A	Column B
_____	**1.** Fraction	**A.** two fractions with the same bottom number
_____	**2.** Simplify	**B.** part of a whole number.
_____	**3.** Numerator	**C.** to express a fraction in lowest terms
_____	**4.** Least common denominator	**D.** a number made up of a whole number and a fraction
_____	**5.** Improper fraction	**E.** product of one fraction's numerator and another fraction's denominator
_____	**6.** Mixed number	**F.** a fraction that has a numerator equal to or larger than the denominator
_____	**7.** Denominator	**G.** the smallest number that will go into two denominators
_____	**8.** Cross product	**H.** bottom number of a fraction that tells how many parts make up one whole
_____	**9.** Common denominators	**I.** top number of a fraction that tells how many parts are used

Part 2
Comparing Fractions

Compare the fractions. Write < (less than), = (equal to), or > (greater than) on the line.

1. $\frac{3}{8}$ _____ $\frac{2}{5}$ **3.** $\frac{1}{2}$ _____ $\frac{5}{11}$ **5.** $\frac{2}{3}$ _____ $\frac{8}{15}$

2. $\frac{9}{10}$ _____ $\frac{18}{20}$ **4.** $\frac{5}{8}$ _____ $\frac{4}{7}$

Part 3
Renaming

Rename each fraction in simplest form.

1. $\frac{20}{50}$ _____   **3.** $\frac{17}{51}$ _____   **5.** $\frac{30}{45}$ _____

2. $\frac{8}{32}$ _____   **4.** $\frac{14}{28}$ _____

Part 4
Improper Fractions and Mixed Numbers

Rename each improper fraction as a mixed number in simplest form.

1. $\frac{42}{8}$ _____   **3.** $\frac{19}{2}$ _____   **5.** $\frac{63}{5}$ _____

2. $\frac{25}{3}$ _____   **4.** $\frac{50}{6}$ _____

Part 5
Multiplying Fractions

Write each product in simplest form.

1. $\frac{7}{8} \times 4$ _____   **3.** $\frac{1}{6} \times 24$ _____   **5.** $\frac{10}{11} \times \frac{22}{30}$ _____

2. $\frac{3}{5} \times \frac{20}{21}$ _____   **4.** $\frac{3}{4} \times \frac{2}{15}$ _____

Part 6
Dividing Fractions

Write the answers in simplest form.

1. $\frac{5}{12} \div \frac{1}{6}$ _____   **3.** $\frac{9}{10} \div \frac{3}{5}$ _____   **5.** $\frac{11}{14} \div \frac{3}{7}$ _____

2. $\frac{7}{8} \div \frac{3}{4}$ _____   **4.** $\frac{23}{24} \div \frac{1}{12}$ _____

Part 7
Adding Fractions

Write the answers in simplest form.

1. $\begin{array}{r} 4\frac{3}{4} \\ + 2\frac{3}{4} \\ \hline \end{array}$ **2.** $\begin{array}{r} 6\frac{2}{3} \\ + 4\frac{1}{3} \\ \hline \end{array}$ **3.** $\begin{array}{r} 8\frac{7}{9} \\ + 1\frac{4}{9} \\ \hline \end{array}$ **4.** $\begin{array}{r} 8\frac{1}{5} \\ + 7\frac{4}{5} \\ \hline \end{array}$ **5.** $\begin{array}{r} \frac{6}{7} \\ + \frac{2}{3} \\ \hline \end{array}$

Part 8
Subtracting Fractions

Write the answer in simplest form.

1. $\begin{array}{r} 13\frac{3}{4} \\ - 6\frac{1}{4} \\ \hline \end{array}$ **2.** $\begin{array}{r} 9\frac{5}{6} \\ - 2\frac{1}{6} \\ \hline \end{array}$ **3.** $\begin{array}{r} 10\frac{7}{8} \\ - 9\frac{1}{8} \\ \hline \end{array}$ **4.** $\begin{array}{r} 9\frac{2}{3} \\ - 5\frac{1}{3} \\ \hline \end{array}$ **5.** $\begin{array}{r} \frac{7}{8} \\ - \frac{3}{4} \\ \hline \end{array}$

Part 9
Solve

Solve each word problem.

1. Anna bought a $4\frac{1}{2}$ pound bag of nuts. She uses $1\frac{3}{4}$ pound for cookies. How many pound of nuts does she have left?

_____

2. Sue has $4\frac{1}{5}$ yards of red fabric and $3\frac{3}{4}$ yards of white fabric. How much fabric does she have altogether?

_____

3. Max bought 8 bags of birdseed. Each bag holds $2\frac{3}{4}$ pounds of seeds. How many total pounds of birdseed does he have?

_____

LESSON 36   What Is a Decimal?

KEY WORDS

Decimal
an amount that
is less than one

Decimal point
a dot that separates
a whole number and
a decimal

Mixed decimal
a number made up
of a whole number
and a decimal

A **decimal** represents an amount that is less than one. A **decimal point** is a dot that separates a whole number from a decimal. A **mixed decimal** is a number that has a whole number and a decimal. The number 42.05 is a mixed decimal. A place value chart helps name the value of a decimal.

Example   What is the place value of **5** in 43.0**5**?

Step 1: Make a place value chart.

Ten-thousands	Thousands	Hundreds	Tens	Ones	Tenths	Hundredths	Thousandths	Ten-thousandths

Step 2: Write the numeral in the chart. Start with the decimal point or dot that separates the whole number and the decimal.

Ten-thousands	Thousands	Hundreds	Tens	Ones	Tenths	Hundredths	Thousandths	Ten-thousandths
			4	3 .	0	5		.

Step 3: Read the name of the column that holds **5**.

Ten-thousands	Thousands	Hundreds	Tens	Ones	Tenths	Hundredths	Thousandths	Ten-thousandths
			4	3 .	0	5		

The digit **5** is in the **hundredths** place. It stands for $\frac{5}{100}$.

Ten-thousands	Thousands	Hundreds	Tens	Ones		Tenths	Hundredths	Thousandths	Ten-thousandths

RULES TO REMEMBER

- When reading a mixed decimal, say "and" for the decimal point.
- When naming a decimal, always state the place name of the last digit.

A Write the name of the place for each underlined digit. Use the place value chart.

1. 17.**6**52 _____

2. 2.14**8** _____

3. 5.046**2** _____

4. 2**6**3.97 _____

5. **9**,381.25 _____

6. 835.**1**74 _____

7. 24.09**3** _____

8. **6**8,954.1 _____

9. 4.628**7** _____

10. 2**1**.96 _____

11. 518.603**7** _____

12. 9.23**6** _____

B Underline the digit that is in the place named.

1. 9.456 (hundredths)

2. 6,804.5 (hundreds)

3. 17.9123 (ten-thousandths)

4. 65,183.29 (ones)

5. 84.0537 (tenths)

6. 6,145.283 (tens)

7. 783.1092 (thousandths)

8. 532,406.78 (ten-thousands)

9. 75.936 (hundredths)

10. 4.8732 (thousandths)

11. 815,263.9 (hundreds)

12. 51.6743 (tenths)

C Write the numeral that means the same as the words.

1. Fifteen and six hundredths _____

2. Ninety-four and fifty-two hundredths _____

3. Six thousand and six thousandths _____

4. Eleven and two hundred thirty-one ten thousandths _____

5. Five and five ten-thousandths _____

LESSON 37 Comparing Decimals

KEY WORDS

Compare
to find the largest
or smallest number

You **compare** decimals when you state that one decimal is larger or smaller than another. In order to name the larger or smaller decimal, you must compare the digits in each decimal place.

Example   Compare 0.421 and 0.45

Step 1: List the decimals you are comparing.
Line up the decimal points.

0.421

0.45

Step 2: Look at the digits in the tenths place.
See if one is greater than the other.

0.421 ◄——┐ Both decimals have a **4**
          │ in the tenths place.
0.45 ◄────┘

Step 3: Look at the digits in the hundredths place.
See if one is greater than the other.

0.421 ◄——┐ **5** is greater than **2**
          │
0.45 ◄────┘ 0.45 > 0.421

0.421 < 0.45   0.421 is less than 0.45

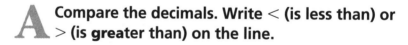 **A** **Compare the decimals. Write < (is less than) or > (is greater than) on the line.**

1. 0.918 _____ 0.9154

2. 0.4 _____ 0.387

3. 0.106 _____ 0.1006

4. 0.23 _____ 0.134

5. 0.708 _____ 0.78

6. 0.5 _____ 0.1555

7. 0.4136 _____ 0.4163

8. 0.275 _____ 0.257

9. 0.1 _____ 0.0999

10. 0.6714 _____ 0.6589

11. 0.32 _____ 0.3201

12. 0.25 _____ 0.2005

13. 0.529 _____ 0.550

14. 0.298 _____ 0.027

15. 0.83 _____ 0.0854

16. 0.006 _____ 0.050

Sometimes you need to compare mixed decimals. Begin by comparing the whole numbers. If they are equal, compare the digits in the tenths place, then the hundredths place.

Example Compare 43.09 and 4.231

Step 1: List the mixed decimals you are comparing.
Line up the decimal points.

43.09
4.231

Step 2: Look at the whole numbers.
See if one is greater than the other.

43.09 ◄─────┐ **43** is greater than **4**
4.231 ◄─────┘

43.09 > 4.231   43.09 is greater than 4.231.

B Compare the mixed decimals. Write < (is less than) or > (is greater than) on the line.

1. 29.35 _____ 117.03

2. 687.1 _____ 686.71

3. 8.229 _____ 2.854

4. 17.22 _____ 21.7

5. 2.009 _____ 1.763

6. 983.2 _____ 988.32

7. 26.714 _____ 26.711

8. 9.205 _____ 9.25

9. 16.3 _____ 163.2

10. 4.286 _____ 4.206

11. 95.41 _____ 95.14

12. 6.3 _____ 6.312

LESSON 38   Rounding Decimals

KEY WORDS

Rounding
renaming a number
as a simpler number

Rounding is renaming a number as a simpler number. Decimals can be rounded to the nearest place.

Example   Round 75.186 to the hundredths place.

Step 1: Find the place you are rounding to.

75.1**8**6   Hundredths place

Step 2: Look at the digit to its right.

75.18**6**   The digit to its right is **6**.

Step 3: If the digit to its right is 5 or more, add 1 to the place you are rounding to. If the digit is less than 5, do not add anything.

75.1**9**6   Since 6 is more than 5, add 1 to the 8 in the hundredths place.

Step 4: Drop all of the digits to the right of the place that you are rounding to.

75.19

75.186 rounded to the hundredths place is **75.19**.

 Round these numbers to the nearest tenth.

1. 44.287 _____

2. 8.324 _____

3. 699.96 _____

4. 51.218 _____

5. 0.379 _____

6. 0.6154 _____

7. 2.34 _____

8. 42.25 _____

9. 14.6458 _____

10. 2.346 _____

Decimals can also be rounded to the nearest whole number.

Example Round 2.8 to the nearest whole number.

Step 1: Look at the last digit to the right of the decimal.

2.**8**   The digit to the right of the decimal is **8**.

Step 2: If the digit to the right of the decimal is 5 or more, add 1 to the whole number. 2.8 Since **8** is more than 5, add 1 to the whole number

3.0

Step 3: Drop the decimal and the digit to the right of the decimal.

2.8 rounded to the nearest whole number is **3**.

B Round these numbers to the nearest hundredth.

1. 70.125 _____

2. 1.2721 _____

3. 8.614 _____

4. 0.892 _____

5. 0.7094 _____

6. 29.106 _____

7. 5.823 _____

8. 2.1239 _____

9. 0.065 _____

10. 2.346 _____

C Round these numbers to the nearest whole number.

1. 4.2 _____

2. 5.5 _____

3. 9.8 _____

4. 12.6 _____

5. 4.3 _____

6. 2.28 _____

7. 7.6 _____

8. 14.17 _____

9. 110.9 _____

10. 227.8 _____

LESSON 39   Adding Decimals

KEY WORDS

Addends
numbers being
added together

Rename
to write a number
as groups of ones
and tens

You add decimals the same way you add whole numbers. The only difference is that you line up the decimal **addends** by their decimal points. Then you find the sum of the digits in each place. If the sum is more than 9, you have to **rename** the number.

Example   What is the sum of 78.5, 3.671, and 14.23?

Step 1: Set up an addition problem.
Line up the addends by their decimal points.

$$
\begin{array}{r}
78.500 \\
3.671 \\
+14.230 \\
\end{array}
$$

— You can add zeros at the end of a decimal.
This helps keep the columns straight.

Step 2: Find the sum of the thousandths column.

$$
\begin{array}{r}
78.500 \\
3.671 \\
+14.230 \\
\hline
1 \\
\end{array}
$$

$0 + 1 + 0 = 1$

Step 3: Find the sum of the hundredths column. Rename if needed.

$$
\begin{array}{r}
1 \\
78.500 \\
3.671 \\
+14.230 \\
\hline
01 \\
\end{array}
$$

$0 + 7 + 3 = 10$
Rename 10 as **1** tenth and **0** hundredths.

Step 4: Find the sum of the tenths column.

$$
\begin{array}{r}
1\,1 \\
78.500 \\
3.671 \\
+14.230 \\
\hline
.401 \\
\end{array}
$$

$1 + 5 + 6 + 2 = 14$
Rename 14 as **1** one and **4** tenths.

Step 5: Find the sum of the ones column.

$$
\begin{array}{r}
11\,1 \\
78.500 \\
3.671 \\
+14.230 \\
\hline
6.401 \\
\end{array}
$$

$1 + 8 + 3 + 4 = 16$
Rename 16 as **1** ten and **6** ones.

Step 6: Find the sum of the tens column.

$$
\begin{array}{r}
11\,1 \\
78.500 \\
3.671 \\
+14.230 \\
\hline
96.401 \\
\end{array}
$$

$1 + 7 + 1 = 9$

The sum is **96.401**.

A Find each sum.

1.	**2.**	**3.**	**4.**	**5.**
45.29	7.38	115.6	93.011	8.66
6.719	45.620	84.29	8.7	85.
+ 3.9	+14.	+ 0.43	+ 5.41	+ 0.837

6.	**7.**	**8.**	**9.**	**10.**
703.2	46.74	1,287.54	65.812	8.965
19.65	839.53	603.	9.14	0.11
+ 2.84	+ 0.405	+ 0.549	+ 3.5	+ 4.44

B Find the sums.

1. 8.19 + 243.771 _____

2. 390.5 + 8.364 _____

3. 2,097.2 + 48.715 _____

4. 9.014 + 553.8 _____

5. 290.6 + 3,354.22 _____

6. 8.15 + 950.387 _____

7. 10.004 + 7.6 _____

8. 918.4 + 37.898 _____

9. 11.112 + 4.5093 _____

10. 6.7 + 389.558 _____

11. 99.56 + 8.314 _____

12. 6.06 + 55.2952 _____

13. 0.602 + 0.35 + 0.4 + 5 _____

14. 25 + 2.5 + 5.02 + 4 _____

15. 3.2 + 9.42 + 0.002 _____

LESSON 40   Subtracting Decimals

KEY WORDS

Difference
the answer to a
subtraction problem

Finding the **difference** of two decimals is just like subtraction of whole numbers. You line up the decimal points and then subtract the digits in each column.

Example   What is 8.092 − 4.13?

Step 1: Set up a subtraction problem. Start with the larger number. Write the smaller number below it so that the decimal points are lined up.

$$\begin{array}{r} 8.092 \\ -4.13\mathbf{0} \\ \hline \end{array}$$ ← Add a zero here to keep the columns straight.

Step 2: Find the difference between the digits in the thousandths place.

$$\begin{array}{r} 8.09\mathbf{2} \\ -4.13\mathbf{0} \\ \hline \mathbf{2} \end{array}$$ $2 - 0 = 2$

Step 3: Find the difference between the digits in the hundredths place.

$$\begin{array}{r} 8.0\mathbf{9}2 \\ -4.1\mathbf{3}0 \\ \hline \mathbf{6}2 \end{array}$$ $9 - 3 = 6$

Step 4: Find the difference between the digits in the tenths place. Regroup if needed.

$$\begin{array}{r} 7\ \mathbf{10} \\ \mathbf{8.0}92 \\ -4.\mathbf{1}30 \\ \hline \mathbf{9}62 \end{array}$$ $10 - 1 = 9$

Step 5: Find the difference between the digits in the ones place.

$$\begin{array}{r} \mathbf{7}\ 10 \\ \mathbf{8.}092 \\ -\mathbf{4.}130 \\ \hline \mathbf{3.}962 \end{array}$$ $7 - 4 = 3\ +$

Check your work by adding:
$$\begin{array}{r} 1 \\ 4.130 \\ 3.962 \\ \hline 8.092 \end{array}$$

$$8.092 - 4.13 = \mathbf{3.962}$$

A Find each difference. Check your work by adding.

1. 3.494
      −1.78

2. 6.28
      −4.7

3. 6.024
      −2.91

4. 1.8
      −0.56

5. 28.9
      −6.84

6. 7.03
      −4.1

7. 55.2
      −28.7

8. 7.25
      −5.1

9. 45.84
      −9.6

10. 1.333
       −0.4

11. 7.5
       −2.0

12. 0.82
       −0.6

13. 9.1
       −8.5

14. 3.4
       −3.2

15. 8.19
       −4.1

16. 0.134
       −0.08

17. 1.22
       −1.1

18. 4.44
       −2.8

19. 0.14
       −0.05

20. 5.6
       −0.6

B Find each difference. Check your work by adding.

1. 78.9 − 45.66 _____

2. 2,910.5 − 7.908 _____

3. 18.09 − 5.442 _____

4. 975.8 − 70.003 _____

5. 13.2 − 1.055 _____

6. 800.4 − 8.404 _____

7. 9.12 − 5.603 _____

8. 411.3 − 8.091 _____

9. 5,768.9 − 43.26 _____

10. 19.99 − 5.613 _____

11. 28 − 1.987 _____

12. 10 − 1.001 _____

LESSON 41 Multiplying Decimals

KEY WORDS

Factors
the numbers that
are multiplied

Product
the answer to a
multiplication problem

You multiply decimals the same way you multiply whole numbers. The only difference is that you must count the number of decimal places in the **factors.** The sum names how many decimal places are in the **product.**

Example What is 18.9 x 4.55?

Step 1: Set up a multiplication problem.
Line the decimal factors up by their last digit.

$$\begin{array}{r} 18.9 \\ \times\,4.55 \\ \hline \end{array}$$

Step 2: Count the number of decimal places in the factors.

$$\begin{array}{r} 18.9 \longleftarrow \text{1 place} \\ \times\,4.55 \longleftarrow \text{2 places} \\ \hline \end{array}$$ The product must have **3** decimal places.

Step 3: Find the first partial product. Regroup as needed.

$$\begin{array}{r} 44 \\ 18.9 \\ \times\,4.55 \\ \hline 9\,45 \end{array}$$ $189 \times 5 = 945$

Step 4: Put a 0 under the last digit in the first partial product.
Then find the next partial product. Regroup as needed.

$$\begin{array}{r} 44 \\ 18.9 \\ \times\,4.55 \\ \hline 9\,45 \\ 94\,50 \end{array}$$ $189 \times 5 = 945$

Step 5: Put a 0 under the last two digits in the first partial product.
Then find the next partial product. Regroup as needed.

$$\begin{array}{r} 33 \\ 18.9 \\ \times\,4.55 \\ \hline 9\,45 \\ 94\,50 \\ 756\,00 \end{array}$$ $189 \times 4 = 756$

Step 6: Find the sum of the partial products. Put a decimal point in the final product so that it has 3 decimal places.

$$\begin{array}{r} 18.9 \\ \times\,4.55 \\ \hline 19\,45 \\ 194\,50 \\ 756\,00 \\ \hline 85.995 \end{array}$$

$18.9 \times 4.55 = \mathbf{85.995}$

A Put the decimal point in the proper place in the product.

1.	3.762 × 1.6 ————— 60192	**2.**	5.134 × 8 ————— 41072	**3.**	157.2 × 5.34 ————— 839448	**4.**	7.05 × 2.3 ————— 16215
5.	3.44 × 1.9 ————— 6536	**6.**	.867 × 2 ————— 1734	**7.**	8.15 × 7.7 ————— 62755	**8.**	46.9 × 3.42 ————— 160398
9.	3.09 × .65 ————— 20085	**10.**	101.4 × 3.78 ————— 383292	**11.**	47.8 × 30.9 ————— 147702	**12.**	9.002 × .611 ————— 5500222

B Multiply to find the product.

1.	3.27 × 1.8	**2.**	9.03 × .24	**3.**	.65 × 3.9	**4.**	8.004 × .16
5.	2.19 × .347	**6.**	72.98 × .413	**7.**	.059 × 2.8	**8.**	6.33 × .51
9.	3.814 × .2	**10.**	6.29 × .451	**11.**	1.09 × 8.78	**12.**	5.33 × .216
13.	2.3 × 4.6	**14.**	2.96 × .17	**15.**	.43 × 1.7	**16.**	5.62 × .17

LESSON 42   Scientific Notation

Scientific notation
a number between one
and ten, including one,
multiplied by a power
of ten

Exponent
a number that tells
how many times
another number is
used as a factor

Negative exponent
an exponent less than
zero; used to express
small numbers

Scientific notation is a way of expressing very large numbers. When using scientific notation to express a large number, move the decimal point to the *left* so that the greatest place is ones. Then write a multiplication sign and 10 with an **exponent** that shows how many times the decimal point was moved.

Example   What is 34,987,000 written in scientific notation?

Step 1: Put a decimal point at the end of the number.

34,987,000.

Then move the decimal point to the *left* so that the greatest place is the ones place.

3.4987000 ◄──── The decimal point was moved **7** places.

Step 2: Drop the zeros after the decimal point. Put a multiplication sign after the decimal.

3.4987 ×

Step 3: Write 10 after the multiplication sign. Write the number of places you moved the decimal point as its **exponent**.

3.4987×10^7 ◄──── An exponent is written above the line.

34,987,000 written in scientific notation is $\mathbf{3.4987 \times 10^7}$

A Write each number in scientific notation.

1. 78,000,000 _____   7. 270,000,000 _____

2. 1,653,200 _____   8. 1,453,900,000 _____

3. 844,300,000 _____   9. 22,800 _____

4. 59,616,890 _____   10. 55,629,810 _____

5. 7,900,000 _____   11. 900,000,000 _____

6. 41,280,000 _____   12. 6,535,000 _____

You can use scientific notation to represent decimals, too. Move the decimal point to the *right* so that the greatest place is ones. Then write a multiplication sign and 10 with a **negative exponent** that shows how many times the decimal point was moved

Example | What is 0.00053 written in scientific notation?

Step 1: Move the decimal point to the *right* so that the greatest place is the ones place.

0.00053
5.3 ◄——————— The decimal point was moved **4** places.

Step 2: Drop the zeros. Put a multiplication sign after the decimal.

5.3 $\times$

Step 3: Write 10 after the multiplication sign. Write the number of places you moved the decimal point as its **negative exponent.**

5.3 $\times$ 10^{-4} ◄——————— An exponent is written above the line.

0.00053 written in scientific notation is 5.3×10^{-4}

B Write each decimal in scientific notation.

1. 0.0038 _____

2. 0.18745 _____

3. 0.075749 _____

4. 0.92 _____

5. 0.00000001 _____

6. 0.001873 _____

7. 0.0005353 _____

8. 0.08129 _____

9. 0.007608 _____

10. 0.0002 _____

11. 0.65203 _____

12. 0.000000008 _____

LESSON 43   Daviding Decimals

KEY WORDS

Dividend
the number that
is being divided

Divisor
the number by which
you are dividing

Quotient
the answer to a
division problem

Dividing a decimal by a whole number is just like dividing whole numbers. The only difference is that you must put a decimal point in the quotient.

Example What is $5.117 \div 17$?

Step 1: Set up a division problem. First write the **dividend.**

5.117

Step 2: Put a division sign around the dividend. Outside the division sign, write the **divisor.**

$17\overline{)5.117}$

Step 3: Divide. Write the quotient above the division sign. Put a decimal point in the quotient directly above its location in the dividend.

$$
\begin{array}{r}
0.301 \\
17\overline{)5.117} \\
5\ 1 \\
\overline{017} \\
17 \\
\overline{0}
\end{array}
$$

$5.117 \div 17 = \mathbf{0.301}$

A Find each quotient.

1. $7\overline{)861}$ 2. $4\overline{)3.216}$ 3. $9\overline{)542.7}$ 4. $8\overline{)2.468}$ 5. $3\overline{)811.2}$

6. $5\overline{)475.5}$ 7. $6\overline{)0.5442}$ 8. $28\overline{)87.92}$ 9. $19\overline{)8.55}$ 10. $37\overline{)36.26}$

11. $41\overline{)34.85}$ 12. $23\overline{)12.88}$ 13. $48\overline{)155.52}$ 14. $79\overline{)410.8}$ 15. $25\overline{)15.575}$

You can divide a decimal by a decimal, too. If the divisor is a decimal, you must move the decimal point to the right to make a whole number. Then you move the decimal point in the dividend the same number of places.

Example   What is $8.544 \div 2.67$?

Step 1: Set up a division problem.

$$2.67{\overline{\smash{\big)}\,8.544}}$$

Step 2: Move the decimal point in the divisor so it becomes a whole number. Move the decimal point in the dividend the same number of places.

$$267{\overline{\smash{\big)}\,854.4}} \longleftarrow \text{You move the decimal point two places.}$$

Step 3: Divide. Write the quotient above the division sign. Put a decimal point in the quotient directly above its location in the dividend.

$$
\begin{array}{r}
3.2 \\
267{\overline{\smash{\big)}\,854.4}} \\
\underline{801} \\
53\ 4 \\
\underline{53\ 4} \\
0
\end{array}
$$

$8.544 \div 2.67 = \mathbf{3.2}$

B Find each quotient.

1. $0.55{\overline{\smash{\big)}\,2.002}}$ **2.** $3.8{\overline{\smash{\big)}\,0.988}}$ **3.** $0.23{\overline{\smash{\big)}\,0.0391}}$ **4.** $5.17{\overline{\smash{\big)}\,33.088}}$

5. $0.04{\overline{\smash{\big)}\,0.348}}$ **6.** $0.29{\overline{\smash{\big)}\,2.1895}}$ **7.** $0.63{\overline{\smash{\big)}\,1.3419}}$ **8.** $4.2{\overline{\smash{\big)}\,2.352}}$

9. $0.17{\overline{\smash{\big)}\,0.0051}}$ **10.** $0.09{\overline{\smash{\big)}\,0.0729}}$ **11.** $3.5{\overline{\smash{\big)}\,10.15}}$ **12.** $0.18{\overline{\smash{\big)}\,0.0396}}$

LESSON 44 Renaming Decimals as Fractions

KEY WORDS

Numerator
the top number of a fraction that tells how many parts are used

Denominator
the bottom number of a fraction that tells the number of parts to the whole

Both a decimal and a fraction name part of a whole. You can rename a decimal as a fraction. The numerator is the decimal without the decimal point. The denominator is the value of the last place of the decimal.

Example | Rename 0.85 as a fraction.

Step 1: Write the decimal without the decimal point as the numerator.

85

Step 2: Write the name of the last place of the decimal as the denominator.

$\frac{85}{100}$ the last place of the decimal is hundredths

Step 3: Simplify the fraction.

$$\frac{85 \div 5}{100 \div 5} = \frac{17}{20}$$

$$0.85 = \frac{17}{20}$$

 Rename each decimal as a fraction. Simplify as needed.

1. 0.12 _____

2. 0.025 _____

3. 0.0004 _____

4. 0.386 _____

5. 0.911 _____

6. 0.426 _____

7. 0.575 _____

8. 0.6142 _____

9. 0.8 _____

10. 0.62 _____

11. 0.325 _____

12. 0.3993 _____

13. 0.009 _____

14. 0.1225 _____

15. 0.7000 _____

You can rename a mixed decimal as a mixed number. Write the whole number part of the mixed decimal as the whole number part of the mixed number. Then rename the decimal as a fraction.

Example Rename 59.242 as a fraction.

Step 1: Write the whole number part of the mixed number.

59

Step 2: Write the decimal without the decimal point as the numerator.

59 242

Step 3: Write the name of the last place of the decimal as the denominator.

$59 \frac{242}{1,000}$

Step 4: Simplify.

$59 \frac{242 \div 2}{1,000 \div 2} = 59 \frac{121}{500}$

$59.242 = 59 \frac{121}{500}$

B Rename each mixed decimal as a mixed number.

1. 4.5 _____

2. 16.075 _____

3. 172.33 _____

4. 9.19 _____

5. 3.0002 _____

6. 18.22 _____

7. 44.006 _____

8. 12.024 _____

9. 5.4455 _____

10. 84.084 _____

11. 250.008 _____

12. 1.001 _____

13. 7.675 _____

14. 816.2 _____

15. 3.0005 _____

LESSON 45   Problem Solving with Decimals

Word problems can describe decimal problems. Read the sentences and then answer the decimal problem.

Example   Carole bought steaks for dinner. The steaks cost $2.85 a pound. She bought 4.8 pounds of steak. Carole paid for the steaks with a $20 bill. How much change did she receive?

Step 1: State the question you must answer. This is often found at the end of a word problem. The question you must answer for this problem is *How much change did Carole receive?*

Step 2: Make a list of the information you are given.

She bought steak for dinner.
The steak cost $2.85 per pound.
She bought 4.8 pounds of steak.
She paid with a $20 bill.

Step 3: Make a plan to solve the problem.

1. Multiply the amount of steaks she bought by the cost per pound.
2. Subtract the product from $20.

Step 4: Follow your plan.

$$\begin{array}{r} 2.85 \\ \times\ 4.8 \\ \hline 2280 \\ 11400 \\ \hline 13680 \end{array} \qquad \begin{array}{r} \$20.00 \\ -\ 13.68 \\ \hline \$6.32 \end{array}$$

13680 ⟶ Insert the decimal point ⟶ $13.68

Carole received **$6.32** in change.

 A **Use the steps to solve each word problem.**

Jill has 14.75 yards of fabric. She wants to divide the fabric into 5 equal pieces. How large will each piece be?

1. State the question you must answer.

2. List what you know.

_____

_____

3. Make a plan to solve the problem.

_____

_____

4. Follow your plan.

Russ earns $8.20 an hour. Last week, Russ worked 32.5 hours. How much money did Russ earn last week?

5. State the question you must answer.

_____

_____

6. List what you know.

_____

_____

7. Make a plan to solve the problem.

_____

_____

8. Follow your plan.

B Use the same steps to solve these problems.

1. Randy drove 371.2 miles to visit his cousin. The trip took him 6.4 hours. What was Randy's average speed?

2. Justin spent $23.95 for jeans, $12.85 for a shirt, and $2.75 for socks. He paid for the items with a $50 bill. How much change did Justin receive?

Part 1
Matching Definitions

Match each word in Column A with its definition in Column B.

Column A	Column B
_____ **1.** Compare	**A.** an amount less than one
_____ **2.** Decimal Point	**B.** numbers that are being multiplied
_____ **3.** Rounding	**C.** a dot that separates whole numbers and decimals
_____ **4.** Mixed decimal	**D.** renaming a number as a simpler number
_____ **5.** Factors	**E.** a number that shows how many times another number is a factor
_____ **6.** Scientific Notation	**F.** finding the largest or smallest number
_____ **7.** Exponent	**G.** a whole number and a decimal.
_____ **8.** Decimal	**H.** a number between one and ten multiplied by a power of ten.

Part 2
Place Value

Write the name of the place for each underlined digit.

1. 89.0<u>5</u>6 _____

2. 317.<u>9</u>5 _____

3. 9.142<u>3</u> _____

4. 5,<u>4</u>78.12 _____

5. 802.74<u>5</u>3 _____

6. 2<u>7</u>1.046 _____

Part 3
Comparing Decimals

Write < (less than), > (greater than), or = (equal to) on the line.

1. .89 _____ .089   **3.** .911 _____ .92   **5.** .311 _____ .4

2. .2 _____ .05   **4.** .500 _____ .5   **6.** .782 _____ .728

Part 4
Rounding Decimals

Round each decimal to the place named in the parentheses.

1. 65.815 (hundredths) _____   **3.** 4,280.74 (hundreds) _____

2. 753.2814 (tenths) _____   **4.** 19.2987 (thousandths) _____

Part 5
Adding Decimals

Find the sum.

1. 45.9 + 374.114 _____   **4.** 36.713 + 655 _____

2. 7,294.03 + 87.2951 _____   **5.** 416.2 + .8368 _____

3. 1.2803 + 67.5 _____   **6.** .663 + .43 _____

Part 6
Subtracting Decimals

Find the difference.

1. 57.19 − 43.08 _____   **4.** 89.3 − 64.6 _____

2. 35.763 − 14.512 _____   **5.** 218.84 − 47.091 _____

3. 695.7 − 325.6 _____   **6.** 13.2 − 1.1 _____

Part 7
Multiplying Decimals

Find the product. Put the decimal point in the proper place.

1. 4.52×27.6 _____   **4.** $7.4 \times .125$ _____

2. 5.61×8.2 _____   **5.** $2.6 \times .003$ _____

3. $6.7 \times .415$ _____   **6.** 6.6×5.13 _____

Part 8
Using Scientific Notation

Write each number in scientific notation.

1. 352,000 _____   **4.** 67,000,000 _____

2. 45,000,000 _____   **5.** 835,000 _____

3. 1,756,000 _____   **6.** 4,195,000,000 _____

Part 9
Dividing Decimals

Divide.

1. $4.2\overline{)23.52}$ **3.** $.913\overline{)4.2911}$ **5.** $1.7\overline{).0034}$

2. $5.17\overline{)341.22}$ **4.** $.006\overline{).054}$ **6.** $.32\overline{)1.152}$

Part 10
Renaming Decimals as Fractions

Rename each decimal as a fraction.
Write the answer in simplest form.

1. .45 _____   **3.** .006 _____   **5.** .054 _____

2. .028 _____   **4.** .125 _____   **6.** .182 _____

LESSON 46

What Is Percent?

KEY WORDS

Percent
part of a whole that is made up of 100 equal sections

A **percent** names part of a whole just as fractions and decimals do. A percent names part of a whole that is divided into 100 equal sections.

Example What percent of the figure is shaded?

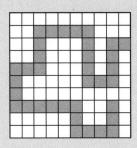

Step 1: Count the number of shaded squares.

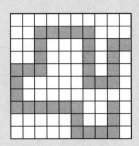 ← **35** squares are shaded

Step 2: Write the number of shaded squares. Then write the percent symbol **%.**

35%

35% of the figure is shaded

A Tell what percent of each figure is shaded. Then tell what percent of the figure is not shaded.

1.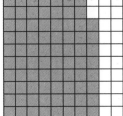

2.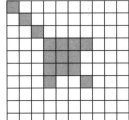

Shaded _____ Not shaded _____   Shaded _____ Not shaded _____

3.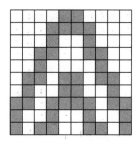

Shaded _____ Not shaded _____

4.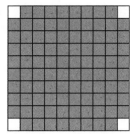

Shaded _____ Not shaded _____

5.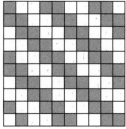

Shaded _____ Not shaded _____

6.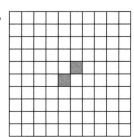

Shaded _____ Not shaded _____

7.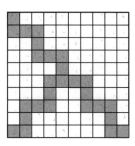

Shaded _____ Not shaded _____

8.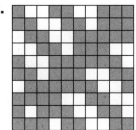

Shaded _____ Not shaded _____

B Rose asked 100 people to name their favorite flavor ice cream. She organized the results in the table. Complete the table by filling in the column marked Percent.

	Flavor	Responses	Percent
1.	Chocolate	37	
2.	Vanilla	28	
3.	Mint	14	
4.	Strawberry	11	
5.	Cookie Dough	10	

LESSON 47   Writing Percents as Decimals and Fractions

A **percent** can be expressed as a decimal. To change a percent to a decimal, remove the % symbol. Put a decimal point at the end of the number. Then move the decimal point two places to the *left* so that the last digit is in the hundredths column.

Example Write 54% as a decimal.

Step 1: Write the percent without the % symbol.

54

Step 2: Put a decimal point at the end of the number.

54.

Move the decimal point two places to the left.

0.54

54% expressed as a decimal is **0.54**.

 Write each percent as a decimal.

1. 78% _____   **9.** 33.3% _____

2. 99% _____   **10.** 12% _____

3. 4.7% _____   **11.** 17.5% _____

4. 91% _____   **12.** 29% _____

5. 62.5% _____   **13.** 1% _____

6. 2% _____   **14.** 25% _____

7. 14% _____   **15.** 66.6% _____

8. 100% _____

A **percent** can be expressed as a fraction. To change a percent to a fraction, remove the % symbol. Write the number as a numerator over a denominator of 100. Simplify if needed.

■ To change a percent to a decimal, drop the % symbol and move the decimal point two places to the left.

| **Example** | Write 54% as a fraction. |

Step 1: Write the percent without the % symbol.

54

Step 2: Write the number as a numerator over a denominator of 100.

$\frac{54}{100}$

Step 3: Simplify.

$\frac{54}{100} = \frac{54 \div 2}{100 \div 2} = \frac{27}{50}$

54% expressed as a fraction is $\frac{27}{50}$

B Write each percent as a fraction.

1. 4% _____

2. 55% _____

3. 12% _____

4. 100% _____

5. 25% _____

6. 85% _____

7. 1% _____

8. 29% _____

9. 3% _____

10. 500% _____

11. 75% _____

12. 96% _____

13. 15% _____

14. 24% _____

15. 46% _____

LESSON 48   Percent Sentences

KEY WORDS

Rate
percent or part of
a whole amount

Base
the whole amount
you are taking a part
or percent of

Percentage
product of multiplying
the rate and the base

A percent sentence describes a relationship between a part and a whole. The **rate** is a percent or part of a whole amount. The **base** is the whole amount. The **percentage** is how much of the whole is being talked about.

Example   Name the rate, base, and percentage in *15% of 60 is 9*.

Step 1: Find the rate. It is written as a percent.

15% of 60 is 9   Since **15%** is written as a percent, it is the **rate**.

Step 2: Find the base. It usually comes after the word *of*.

15% **of 60** is 9   **60** is the whole amount. It is the **base**.

Step 3: Find the percentage. It usually comes just before or just after the word *is*.

15% of 60 **is 9**   **9** is the **percentage**. It is the product of the rate and base.

A Name the rate, base, and percentage in each percent statement.

1. 28% of 50 is 14.   Rate _____ Base _____ Percentage_____

2. 75% of 102 is 76.5. Rate _____ Base _____ Percentage_____

3. 13% of 60 is 7.8.   Rate _____ Base _____ Percentage_____

4. 95% of 300 is 285. Rate _____ Base _____ Percentage_____

5. 2% of 54 is 1.08.   Rate _____ Base _____ Percentage_____

Some word problems contain a percent sentence with a missing part. In order to solve the problem, you must determine whether the rate, base, or percentage is missing.

Example 72 is 50% of what number?

Step 1: Identify the two parts of a percent sentence contained in the problem.

72 is **50%** of what number?

—————The % shows that 50% is the rate.

The word *is* shows that 72 is the percentage.

Step 2: Name the missing part.

You know the rate.
You know the percentage.
The base is missing.

B Read each percent sentence. State whether the rate, base, or percentage is missing.

1. What is 18% of $52.50? _____

2. 24 is 50% of what number? _____

3. 75 is what percent of 300? _____

4. What is 35% of 40? _____

5. 22 is what percent of 88? _____

6. 12.8 is 40% of what number? _____

7. What is 29% of 150? _____

8. 83 is what percent of 415? _____

9. 45% of what number is 40.5? _____

10. What is 250% of 32? _____

LESSON 49   Finding Percentages

KEY WORDS

Rate
percent or part of
a whole amount

Base
the whole amount
you are taking a part
or percent of

Percentage
product of multiplying
the rate and the base

Sometimes you must identify the percentage in order to solve a percent problem. You can find the **percentage** by expressing the **rate** as a decimal. Then multiply the decimal by the **base.**

Example   5% of 60 is what number?

Step 1: Write the rate as a decimal.

5% = **0.05** ←——— To write a percent as a decimal, remove the % symbol. Put a decimal point at the end of the number. Then move the decimal point two places to the left.

Step 2: Multiply the decimal by the base.

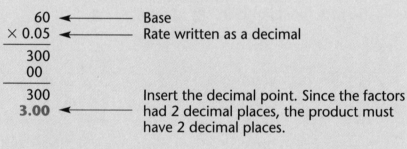

```
       60  ←——————— Base
    × 0.05  ←——————— Rate written as a decimal
    ------
      300
       00
    ------
      300
     3.00  ←——————— Insert the decimal point. Since the factors
                     had 2 decimal places, the product must
                     have 2 decimal places.
```

5% of 60 is **3**

A Find the percentage.

1. 45% of 80 is _____

2. 75% of 68 is _____

3. 4% of 35 is _____

4. 6.5% of 70 is _____

5. 18% of 55 is _____

6. 36% of 90 is _____

7. 12% of 25 is _____

8. 88% of 40 is _____

9. 55% of 96 is _____

10. 200% of 17 is _____

11. 42% of 60 is _____

12. 2.5% of 34 is _____

RULES TO REMEMBER

■ A percentage is the product of a rate and a base.

■ The order in which you write your factors does not affect the product. So, you can write either the rate or the base first.

B Solve for the percentage.

1. What number is 28% of 52? _____

2. 50% of 62 is what number? _____

3. What number is 45% of 300? _____

4. What number is 17% of 92? _____

5. 40% of 55 is what number? _____

6. 15% of 24 is what number? _____

7. What is 29% of 45? _____

8. What is 0.5% of 84? _____

9. 25% of 45 is what number? _____

10. What is 30% of 74? _____

11. 25% of 72 is what number? _____

12. What is 39% of 10? _____

LESSON 50   Finding the Base

KEY WORDS

Rate
percent or part of
a whole amount

Base
the whole amount
you are taking a part
or percent of

Percentage
product of multiplying
the rate and the base

Sometimes you must identify the base in order to solve a percent problem. You can find the **base** by expressing the **rate** as a decimal. Then divide the percentage by the decimal.

Example   15% of what number is 9?

Step 1: Express the rate as a decimal.

15% = 0.15 ◄——— To write a percent as a decimal, remove the % symbol. Put a decimal point at the end of the number. Then move the decimal point two places to the left.

Step 2: Divide the percentage by the decimal.

Move the decimal point two places to the right to make the divisor a whole number.

$$
\begin{array}{r}
60 \\
15.\overline{)900} \\
90 \\
\hline
00
\end{array}
$$

◄——— Put a decimal point at the end of the dividend. Move it two places also. Add zeros to fill the places.

9 is 15% of **60**

 Find the base.

1. 25% of _____ is 24.

2. 80% of _____ is 36.8.

3. 16% of _____ is 6.4.

4. 30% of _____ is 21.

5. 55% of _____ is 22.

6. 6% of _____ is 2.88.

7. 2% of _____ is 1.32.

8. 75% of _____ is 375.

9. 11% of _____ is 9.9.

10. 45% of _____ is 8.55.

11. 20% of _____ is 13.2.

12. 1.5% of _____ is 1.8.

B Solve for the base.

1. 54% of what number is 108? _____

2. 35% of what number is 21? _____

3. 4.5% of what number is 0.45? _____

4. 12% of what number is 8.4? _____

5. 40% of what number is 33? _____

6. 5% of what number is 8? _____

7. 29% of what number is 87? _____

8. 1% of what number is 4.7? _____

9. 25% of what number is 13? _____

10. 80% of what number is 89.6? _____

11. 16% of what number is 32? _____

12. 84% of what number is 63? _____

LESSON 51 Finding the Rate

KEY WORDS

Rate
percent or part of a whole amount

Base
the whole amount you are taking a part or percent of

Percentage
product of multiplying the rate and the base

Sometimes you need to find the **rate** to solve a percent problem. You can find the rate by dividing the **percentage** by the **base.**

Example What percent of 24 is 6?

Step 1: Express the base as a decimal.

$$24 = 0.24$$ ← To write the base as a decimal, put a decimal point at the end of the number. Then move the decimal point two places to the left.

Step 2: Divide the percentage by the decimal.

Move the decimal point two places to the right to make the divisor a whole number. ⟶

```
          25
   24,) 600.
        48
       ----
       120
      -120
       ----
         0
```

← Put a decimal point at the end of the dividend. Move it two places also.

6 is **25%** of 24

A Find the rate.

1. _____ % of 18 is 5.4.

2. _____ % of 90 is 58.5.

3. _____ % of 150 is 112.5.

4. _____ % of 40 is 2.

5. _____ % of 50 is 22.

6. _____ % of 72 is 11.52.

7. _____ % of 36 is 4.32.

8. _____ % of 48 is 1.92.

9. _____ % of 26 is 3.9.

10. _____ % of 80 is 36.

11. _____ % of 47 is 2.35.

12. _____ % of 20 is 50.

B Solve for the rate.

1. What percent of 38 is 2.28? _____

2. What percent of 21 is 7? _____

3. What percent of 54 is 10.8? _____

4. What percent of 46 is 36.8? _____

5. What percent of 51 is 5.1? _____

6. What percent of 19 is 0.38? _____

7. What percent of 25 is 37.5? _____

8. What percent of 4 is 3? _____

9. What percent of 70 is 25.2? _____

10. What percent of 300 is 33? _____

11. What percent of 50 is 17.5? _____

12. What percent of 96 is 35.52? _____

LESSON 52   Problem Solving with Percents

KEY WORDS

Rate
percent or part of
a whole amount

Base
the whole amount
you are taking a part
or percent of

Percentage
product of multiplying
the rate and the base

Word problems can describe percent problems. Read
the sentences and then write the percent problem.

Example   Jim has saved $186.00. He spent $70.68 on new
clothes. What percent of his savings did Jim spend?

Step 1: State the question you must answer. This is often found
at the end of a word problem. The question you must
answer for this problem is *What percent of his savings
did Jim spend?*

Step 2: Make a list of the information you are given.

He saved $186.00 ◄——— *$186.00 is the base.*
He spent $70.68. ◄——— *$70.68 is the percentage.*

Step 3: Make a plan to solve the problem.

1. Write the base as a decimal.
2. Divide the percentage by the base.
3. Find the rate.

Step 4: Follow your plan.

$186 ——► 1.86 ——► Write the base as a decimal.

$$\begin{array}{r} 38 \\ 186\overline{)7068} \\ 558 \\ \hline 1488 \\ -1488 \\ \hline 0 \end{array}$$ Divide the percentage by the base.

Since rate is a percent, add % after the quotient.
Jim spent **38%** of his savings on clothes.

 Use the steps to solve each word problem.

The Hawks won 48% of their soccer games. The team won
12 games. How many games did the Hawks play?

  1. State the question you must answer.

2. List what you know.

_____

_____

3. Make a plan to solve the problem.

_____

_____

4. Follow your plan.

Anne makes a car payment of $130.00 each month. The payment is 20% of her monthly salary. How much does Anne earn each month?

5. State the question you must answer.

_____

_____

6. List what you know.

_____

_____

7. Make a plan to solve the problem.

_____

_____

8. Follow your plan.

B Use the same steps to solve these problems.

1. The distance between Kathy's house and Spring Lake is 378 miles. Kathy has driven 132.3 miles. What percent of the distance has she driven?

2. On Monday, a factory made 950 zippers. A supervisor found that 4% of the zippers were broken. How many zippers were broken?

UNIT TEST

Part 1
Matching Definitions

Match each word in Column A with its definition in Column B.

Column A | Column B

_____ **1.** Base   **A.** Part of a whole that contains a numerator and a denominator

_____ **2.** Decimal   **B.** percent or part of a whole amount

_____ **3.** Fraction   **C.** product of multiplying the rate and the base

_____ **4.** Percent   **D.** the whole amount you are taking a part or percentage of

_____ **5.** Percentage   **E.** part of a whole made up of 100 equal sections

_____ **6.** Rate   **F.** an amount that is less than one and contains digits and a decimal point

Part 2
Meaning of Percent

Tell what percent of the figure is shaded and what percent is unshaded.

1.   **2.**

Shaded _____ Unshaded _____   Shaded _____ Unshaded _____

Part 3
Writing Percents as Decimals and Fractions

Write each percent as a decimal or a fraction

1. 86% _____   **3.** 22% _____   **5.** 61% _____

2. 5% _____   **4.** 98% _____

Write each percent as a fraction in simplest form.

6. 48% _____   **8.** 16% _____   **10.** 2% _____

7. 25% _____   **9.** 150% _____

Part 4
Finding Percentages

Find the percentage.

1. 25% of 76 is _____

2. 14% of 50 is _____

3. 85% of 200 is _____

4. 32% of 44 is _____

5. 75% of 144 is _____

6. 150% of 54 is _____

Part 5
Finding Bases

Find the base.

1. 42% of _____ is 25.2

2. 18% of _____ is 9

3. 75% of _____ is 225

4. 5% of _____ is 1.25

5. 150% of _____ is 18

6. 38% of _____ is 34.2

Part 6
Finding Rates

Find the rate.

1. _____% of 150 is 45

2. _____% of 20 is 2.8

3. _____% of 250 is 187.5

4. _____% of 60 is 57

5. _____% of 50 is 16.5

6. _____% of 88 is 4.4

Part 7
Solve each
word problem.

1. If 70% is a passing grade, then how many questions do you need to answer correctly to pass a 60 question test?

_____

2. Al bought a used car for $5,400. He put down $1,620. What percent of the total cost was his down payment?

_____

3. There are 168 males and 72 females in the Oakdale Soccer Club. What percent of the club is females?

_____

4. Nate earned $220.00 last week. He put $61.60 in a savings account. What percent of his pay did Nate save?

_____

5. Last year, a basketball team won 45% of its games. The team played 60 games. How many games did the team win?

_____

LESSON 53   Points, Lines and Angles

KEY WORDS

Geometry
the study of points, lines, angles, surfaces, and solids

Point
a location in space shown by a dot

Line
a set of many points that extend in opposite directions

Line segment
a part of a line with two endpoints

Ray
a line with a beginning point but no end

Angle
a figure made up of two sides or rays with the same endpoint

Geometry is the study of points, lines, angles, surfaces and solids. Knowing the meaning of the Key Words above will help your understand geometry.

Example   Study the key words. Name each drawing.

Step 1: Look at Drawing 1. It is made up of two rays that share an endpoint. It is an **angle.**

Step 2: Look at Drawing 2. It shows part of a line. It has two endpoints. It is a **line segment.**

Step 3: Look at Drawing 3. It is a single dot showing one location in space. It is a **point.**

Step 4: Look at Drawing 4. It shows a line with a beginning point but no end. It is a **ray.**

Step 5: Look at Drawing 5. It is a set of points that extends in opposite directions. It is a **line.**

A Draw a figure to match each name.

1. Point	**2.** Ray

3. Line

4. Line segment

5. Angle

In geometry, different figures are named in different ways.

A **point** is named with one letter. •D is read as "point D."

A **line** is named by any two points on it. Two capital letters with a double arrow above them: $\overleftrightarrow{ST}$ is read as "line ST."

A **line segment** is named by its endpoints. Two capital letters with a line above them: $\overline{AB}$ is read as "line segment AB."

A **ray** is named by its endpoint and a point on it, or two capital letters. $\overrightarrow{AB}$ is read as "ray AB."

An **angle** is named by three capital letters with an $\angle$ in front. The first and last letters are points on the angle. The middle letter names the common endpoint of the rays that form the angle. $\angle RST$ is read as "angle RST"

B Name each figure.

1.
J   K

_____

2. • M

_____

3. •———————•
B   C

_____

4.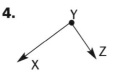
Y
X   Z

_____

5. ←—•———•—→
G   H

_____

LESSON 54 Polygons

A closed figure with three or more sides is a **polygon.** Polygons are named according to the number of sides they have.

Example What is the name of this polygon?

Step 1: Count the number of sides.

Step 2: Look at the table below. It shows that a polygon with five sides is called a pentagon.

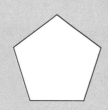

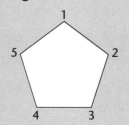

The drawing shows a **pentagon**.

Number of Sides	Name of Polygon
3	Triangle
4	Quadrilateral
5	Pentagon
6	Hexagon
7	Heptagon
8	Octagon

 Write the name for each polygon.

1.
_____

2.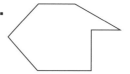
_____

3.
_____

4.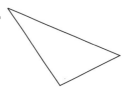
_____

5.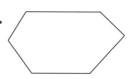
_____

6.
_____

Some figures are three-dimensional. They have height, length, and width. These are called **solid figures.** There are different kinds of solid figures. The drawings below show some solid figures.

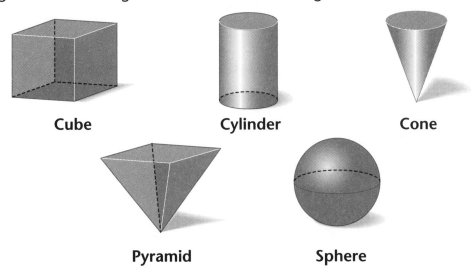

| Cube | Cylinder | Cone |

| Pyramid | Sphere |

RULES TO REMEMBER

■ Solid figures have height, length, and width.

■ Polygons are named according to the number of sides they have.

Example   What is the name of this solid figure?

Step 1: Look at the figure. Circles form its top and bottom. A curved surface forms its sides.

Circular bases

Step 2: Look at the drawings above. The drawing of a cylinder has the same traits.

The solid figure is a **cylinder.**

B Name the solid figure each object represents.

1.

_____

2.

_____

3.

_____

4.

_____

5.

_____

6.

_____

LESSON 55 Units of Measurement

Length
the distance from one end to the other end

Customary measurement
system of measurement used in the U.S.

Metric system
system of measurement used in many parts of the world

Customary System of Measurement

12 inches = 1 foot (ft)

36 inches = 1 yard (yd)

3 feet = 1 yard (yd)

1 mile (mi) = 5,280 feet (ft)

1 mile (mi) = 1,760 yards (yd)

Length is the distance from one end of something to the other end. In the United States, length is measured in inches, feet, yards, and miles. This is called **customary measurement**.

Example Sarah jogged 4 miles this week. How many feet did Sarah jog?

Step 1: Use the chart in the outside column. If you are changing from a larger unit (miles) to a smaller unit (feet), multiply.

1 mile > 1 foot

Step 2: Multiply the number of miles Sarah jogged by the number of feet in one mile.

$$\begin{array}{r} 13 \\ 5280 \\ \times\quad 4 \\ \hline 21{,}120 \end{array}$$ Number of feet in 1 mile
Number of miles Sarah jogged

Sarah jogged **21,120 feet.**

Example Brett has 168 inches of wire. How many feet of wire does Brett have?

Step 1: If you are changing from a smaller unit (inches) to a larger unit (feet), divide.

1 inch < 1 foot

Step 2: Divide the number of inches of wire Brett has by the number of inches in one foot.

$$\begin{array}{r} 14 \\ 12\overline{)168} \\ 12 \\ \hline 48 \\ 48 \\ \hline 0 \end{array}$$ Number of inches of wire Brett has

Brett has **14 feet** of wire.

A Change each measure.

1. 5 mi = _____ yd   **2.** 15,840 ft = _____ mi   **3.** 10 mi = _____ ft

4. 144 in. = ____ yd   **5.** 13 yd = ____ ft   **6.** 45 ft = ____ yd

7. 7 yd = ____ ft   **8.** 108 in. = ____ ft   **9.** 11 ft = ____ in.

Many parts of the world use the metric system of measurement. In this system, length is measured in millimeters, centimeters, meters, and kilometers.

RULES TO REMEMBER

■ When changing from a larger unit to a smaller unit, multiply.

■ When changing from a smaller unit to a larger unit, divide.

Example   Carol bought 4 meters of cloth.
How many centimeters of cloth did she buy?

Step 1: Use the metric chart. If you are changing from a larger unit (meter) to a smaller unit (centimeter), multiply.

1 meter $>$ 1 centimeter

Step 2: Multiply the number of meters of cloth Carol bought by the number of centimeters in one meter.

$$\begin{array}{r} 100 \\ \times\ \ 4 \\ \hline 400 \end{array}$$ Number of centimeters in 1 meter
Number of meters of cloth Carol bought

Carol bought **400 centimeters** of cloth.

Example   Ed has 5,500 millimeters of rope.
How many meters of rope does Ed have?

Step 1: If you are changing from a smaller unit (millimeters) to a larger unit (meters), divide.

1 millimeter $<$ 1 meter

Step 2: Divide the number of millimeters of rope Ed has by the number of millimeters in one meter.

$$\begin{array}{r} 5.5 \\ 1000\overline{)5500.0} \\ \underline{5000} \\ 500\ 0 \\ \underline{500\ 0} \\ 0 \end{array}$$ Number of millimeters of rope Ed has

Ed has **5.5 meters** of rope.

Metric System of Measurement

10 millimeters (mm) = 1 centimeter (cm)

1,000 millimeters (mm) = 1 meter (m)

100 centimeters (cm) = 1 meter (m)

1,000 meters (m) = 1 kilometer (km)

B Change each measure.

1. 7 km = ____ m   **2.** 8,500 m = ____ km   **3.** 13 m = ____ cm

4. 400 cm = ____ m   **5.** 3 m = ____ mm   **6.** 4.5 cm = ____ mm

7. 7 cm = ____ mm   **8.** 80 mm = ____ cm   **9.** 250 cm = ____ m

LESSON 56 Measuring Perimeter and Area

Perimeter
the distance around
the outside of a
closed figure

Area
the amount of space
inside a closed figure

Perimeter is the distance around the outside of a closed figure. To find the perimeter of a rectangle, add the length and width, then multiply by 2.
Perimeter $P = 2(l + w)$

Area is the amount of space inside a closed figure. It is measured in square units. To find the area of a rectangle, multiply the length by the width.
Area $A = l \times w$

Example What is the perimeter of this rectangle?

Perimeter

width = 5 in.
length = 8 in.

Step 1: Remember the rule for finding perimeter. $P = 2(l + w)$

Step 2: Add the length and the width $8 + 5 = 13$

Step 3: Multiply by 2 $13 \times 2 = 26$

The **perimeter** of the rectangle is **26 inches**.

Example What is the area of this rectangle?

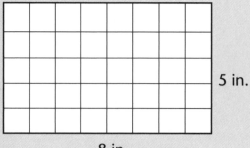

Area

5 in.

8 in.

Step 1: Remember the rule for finding area. $A = l \times w$

Step 2: Multiply the length by the width. $8 \times 5 = 40$

The **area** of the rectangle is **40 square inches**.

A Find the perimeter of each closed figure. P = 2(l + w)

1. 7 ft

7 ft

_____

2. 5 in.

9 in.

_____

3. 2 yd

1.5 yd

_____

4. 14 yd

7 yd

_____

5. 9 ft

9 ft

_____

6. 8 yd

3 yd

_____

B Find the area of each rectangle. A = (l × w)

1. 7 yd

5 yd

_____

2. 4 yd

2 yd

_____

3. 12 yd

15 yd

_____

4. 6 in

6 in

_____

5. 34 yd

6 yd

_____

6. 8 ft

8 ft

_____

UNIT TEST

Part 1
Matching Definitions

Match each word in Column A with its definition in Column B.

Column A	Column B
_____ **1.** Angle	**A.** a part of a line with two endpoints
_____ **2.** Area	**B.** a closed figure with three or more sides
_____ **3.** Length	**C.** the space inside a closed figure
_____ **4.** Line	**D.** a polygon with four sides
_____ **5.** Line segment	**E.** the distance from one end to the other end
_____ **6.** Perimeter	**F.** two sides or rays with a common endpoint
_____ **7.** Triangle	**G.** the distance around the outside of a closed figure
_____ **8.** Polygon	**H.** set of many points that extend in opposite directions
_____ **9.** Quadrilateral	**I.** a polygon with three sides
_____ **10.** Customary measurement	**J.** system of measurement used in the United States

Part 2
Polygons

Write the name of each polygon.

1. A polygon with 5 sides is a _____

2. A polygon with 6 sides is a _____

3. A polygon with 8 sides is a _____

Part 3
Solid Figures

Write the name of each solid figure.

1. 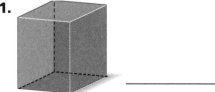 _____

2. 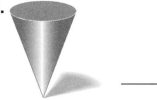 _____

Part 3
Solid Figures, *continued*

3.  _____

4.  _____

Part 4
Measuring Length

Change each unit of length.

1. 48 inches = _____ feet   **4.** 8 km = _____ m

2. 2 miles = _____ yards   **5.** 200 cm = _____ m

3. 12 yards = _____ feet   **6.** 50 mm = _____ cm

Part 5
Perimeter

Find the perimeter of each figure.

1.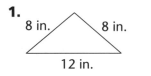
8 in.   8 in.
12 in.
_____

2.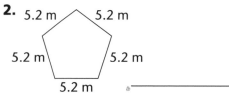
5.2 m   5.2 m
5.2 m   5.2 m
5.2 m   _____

3.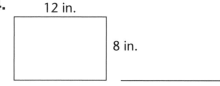
6 in.
6 in.
_____

4.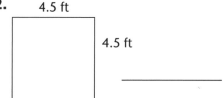
12 in.
8 in.
_____

Part 6
Area

Find the area of each figure.

1.
6.2 in.
6.2 in.
_____

2.
4.5 ft
4.5 ft
_____

3.
14 ft
12 ft
_____

4.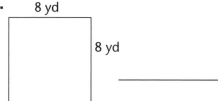
8 yd
8 yd
_____

GLOSSARY

Addition combining numbers to find their total

Addend a number being added to another number

Angle a figure made up of two sides or rays with a common endpoint

Area the amount of space inside a closed figure

Average the number found by dividing the sum of two or more quantities by the number of quantities

Base the number that is used as a factor; the whole amount you are taking a part or percent of

Calculator tool used to perform math operations

Common denominators fractions with the same denominator or bottom number

Common factors for any two numbers, all the numbers that divide evenly into both numbers

Compare to find the largest or smallest number

Cross product product of the numerator of one fraction and the denominator of another fraction

Customary measurement system of measurement used in the U.S.

Decimal an amount that is less than one

Decimal point a dot that separates a whole number and a decimal

Denominator the bottom number of a fraction that tells the number of parts to the whole

Difference the answer to a subtraction problem

Digit one of the characters used to write a numeral

Dividend the number that is being divided

Division finding how many times a number is contained in another number

Divisor the number by which you are dividing

Estimate an answer that is close to the exact answer

Exponent a number that tells how many times another number is used as a factor

Factors the numbers that are multiplied

Fraction part of a whole number

Geometry the study of points, lines, angles, surfaces, and solids

Greatest common factor the largest factor of two numbers

Improper fraction a fraction with a numerator that is equal to or larger than the denominator

Invert to change positions

Least common denominator the smallest number that will go into two denominators

Least common multiple the smallest number that two numbers will divide

Length the distance from one end to the other end

Like fractions fractions with the same denominator

Line a set of many points that extend in opposite directions

Line segment a part of a line with two endpoints

Metric system system of measurement used in many parts of the world

GLOSSARY

Mixed decimal a number made up of a whole number and a decimal

Mixed number a number made up of a whole number and a fraction

Multiple the product of a given number and a whole number

Multiplication adding one number to itself many times

Negative exponent an exponent less than zero; used to express small numbers

Numerator the top number of a fraction that tells how many parts are used

Order to arrange from smallest to largest

Order of operations correct way to complete a number statement that has several operations

Partial product product of one factor and a digit in another factor

Percent part of a whole that is made up of 100 equal sections

Percentage product of multiplying the rate and the base

Perimeter the distance around the outside of a closed figure

Place Value amount a digit is worth based on where it is in a numeral

Point a location in space shown by a dot

Polygon a closed figure with three or more sides

Product the answer to a multiplication problem

Quadrilateral a polygon with four sides

Quotient the answer to a division problem

Rate percent or part of a whole amount

Ray a line with a beginning point but no end

Remainder amount left over when dividing

Rename to write a number as groups of ones and tens

Rounding renaming a number as a simpler number

Scientific notation a number between one and ten, including one, multiplied by a power of ten

Simplest form a fraction in which the numerator and denominator have no common factor greater than 1

Simplify to express in simplest, or lowest, terms

Solid figure a figure that has height, length, and width

Subtraction taking one number away from another to find the difference

Sum the answer to an addition problem

Triangle a polygon with three sides

Unlike fractions fractions that have different denominators

Whole number numbers such as 0, 1, 2, 3, 4, 5

Word problem sentences that describe a math problem

Zero the first whole number

MULTIPLICATION TABLE

×	2	3	4	5	6	7	8	9	10	11	12
2	4	6	8	10	12	14	16	18	20	22	24
3	6	9	12	15	18	21	24	27	30	33	36
4	8	12	16	20	24	28	32	36	40	44	48
5	10	15	20	25	30	35	40	45	50	55	60
6	12	18	24	30	36	42	48	54	60	66	72
7	14	21	28	35	42	49	56	63	70	77	84
8	16	24	32	40	48	56	64	72	80	88	96
9	18	27	36	45	54	63	72	81	90	99	108
10	20	30	40	50	60	70	80	90	100	110	120
11	22	33	44	55	66	77	88	99	110	121	132
12	24	36	48	60	72	84	96	108	120	132	144